That Patchwork Place®

SEASONED with QUILTS

Retta Warehime

Credits

Editor-in-Chief	Barbara Weiland
Technical Editor	Laura M. Reinstatler
Managing Editor	Greg Sharp
Copy Editor	Tina Cook
Proofreader	Leslie Phillips
Text Designer	Dani Ritchardson
Cover Designer	Judy Petry
Production Assistant	Shean Bemis
Photographer	Brent Kane
Technical Illustrator	Laurel Strand
Illustration Assistant	Lisa McKenney
Decorative Art	Maureen Foster

Seasoned with Quilts
©1995 by Retta Warehime
That Patchwork Place, Inc., PO Box 118, Bothell, WA 98041-0118 USA

Printed in the United States of America
00 99 98 97 96 95   6 5 4 3 2 1

Library of Congress Cataloging-in-Publication Data
Warehime, Retta
     Seasoned with quilts / Retta Warehime.
         p.   cm.
     ISBN 1-56477-078-8
     1. Quilting. I. Title
TT835.W357 1995
746.46—dc20   94-48615
                                                        CIP

Dedication

To Dan, Shawna, Jayme, Marci, and Gregg. Thank you for your support and patience. Without you this wouldn't have happened.

Acknowledgments

This book would not have been possible without help from many people. I want to thank:

My family—Dan, Shawna, Jayme, Marci, and Gregg; my sisters, DeeDee and Kathy; and Chris Levernier. These people have been my support group through thick and thin!

Vi McDonald, who has done my hand quilting since I began piecing; her creative ideas always make my work look better! Chris Mewhinney and Donna Thorne for pitching in with their beautiful hand quilting.

Diana Arkell, Debbie Baalman, Beth Cameron, Jackie Gest-Easton, Maureen Foster, Mary Lynn Konyu, Rozan Meacham, Kim Penttila, Angela Poole, and the members of Piecing in the Pines quilt group for their help in "test driving" the patterns. It's hard to find one's own mistakes (or admit they were made), so these wonderful people found them for me.

Kathy Renzelman for her expert painting knowledge and help in making and designing the floorcloths.

Jackie Gest-Easton for all her help with the computer work.

Terry Guizzo and Barbara Ward, owners of Pieceable Dry Goods, and their wonderful customers! Terry and Barb always take time out to answer my questions, help me organize my ideas, and let me use their shop for whatever I might need.

Jackie Wolff, owner of The Quilting Bee, for support, fabric, and teaching the first piecing class I took. If I must blame my habit on someone, it would have to be Jackie.

All my special friends from the past and present, who share their support, enthusiasm, and ideas, never asking for anything in return: Catie Senske, Valeria Hunter, Ann Wiesbeck, MaryLou Larmey, Debbie Mumm, Ryan and Jeri Lynn Liechety, Colleen Medchill, Sue Dixon, Camille Cremin, Deb Jennings, and Carla O'Malley.

My parents, Charles and Marlene Whitney, and my husband's parents, Royal and JoAnn DeBore.

Everyone at That Patchwork Place, one of the best things to happen to the quilting industry.

Contents

"Only from the toils of hard work and the help of family shall the success that is sought for be found."

Retta heard this statement years ago and wholeheartedly agrees. Only with 100% support from her husband, Dan, who cooks six nights a week, and her four children, Shawna, Jayme, Marci, and Gregg (who, by the way, would be happy if they never had to stuff another pattern bag or glue another picture again), has Retta been able to enjoy her successes. With their help, she devotes ten hours a day to sewing, designing, and managing her pattern business, Sew Cherished.

Retta loves designing and piecing. Wherever she goes, everything she sees brings ideas for new patterns. While Retta likes her work to have a distinctive look, she tries not to limit herself. She seeks variety through fabrics, having a special love for plaids, stripes, and dark colors.

Retta's mother introduced her to sewing, and through her patient instruction Retta's skills grew, first with clothing, then crafts, and finally piecing. Classes at a local quilt shop fine-tuned Retta's excellent piecing skills. In classes she reached beyond her routine methods, discovering up-to-date techniques and equipment. Most important, she met other sewers. They taught her to be innovative, and she learned from their creativity.

One step led to another. Retta began assisting at classes, then teaching some of her own. Next, she began to receive custom piecing orders. The custom projects often required different colors and designs than she used for her own projects, stretching her skills and stimulating new ideas. This led her to draft her own patterns, which became the basis for her pattern business.

Retta's journey, from her start in quiltmaking to the point where she finds herself today, meant overcoming hurdles and frustrations along the way. In this book, she hopes to ease some of the frustrations for her readers and to make a contribution to the quilting community that has given so much to her.

Introduction

To finish any project, you have to start! Today, starting a quilt is easy with quick-cutting and speed-piecing techniques. These methods save valuable time and help you to produce more quilts.

The following pages introduce a quick-piecing method for sewing angled seams, Template-Free™ Angled Piecing, as well as a method for making bias-rectangle units. There are simple illustrations to help you lay out, construct, and complete projects more quickly and easily than ever before.

Before beginning a project, read the "Materials and Supplies" and "General Techniques" sections to familiarize yourself with the tools and methods used throughout this book. Then examine the section on color and fabric selection to get tips on planning and choosing materials for your projects.

If you enjoy the comfortable style of country decorating, you will love the section on the design and construction of canvas floorcloths. Painted quilt designs on floorcloths create a warmth similar to the sight of an old quilt on a bed. Now you can start to have fun!

Rotary Cutter and Mat

All the pieced projects in *Seasoned with Quilts* are Template-Free, so you only need to rotary-cut strips, then crosscut the strips into smaller pieces ready to sew into a quilt.

A rotary cutter enables you to quickly cut strips and pieces without templates. For Template-Free cutting, a rotary cutter is easier to handle than scissors and more accurate. There are three blade sizes available. Choose the one most comfortable for you.

A cutting mat is a necessity. A self-healing mat with a rough finish helps hold fabric in place and protects both the blade and the table on which you are cutting. An 18" x 24" mat allows you to cut the long strips called for in this book.

If you are unfamiliar with rotary-cutting equipment, ask a quilter friend or the local quilt shop for a demonstration.

Cutting Guides

You need a ruler to measure fabric and guide the rotary cutter. There are many appropriate rulers, but a favorite is the 24"-long Rotary Rule™. It is made of $\frac{1}{8}$"-thick acrylic plastic and includes lines for cutting strips, lines for 45° and 60° angles, and marks in $\frac{1}{4}$" increments along the edge. The Rotary Mate™ is a 12"-long cutting guide with the same features. There are other rulers to consider as well. Use the BiRangle™ ruler to cut bias-rectangle units, and try the Bias Square® ruler for squaring up corners of quilts and the ends of fabric as you prepare to cut strips. All these cutting guides are available at local quilt shops or from That Patchwork Place. As your skills progress, you may wish to try other rulers.

Sewing Machine

Use a straight-stitch machine in good working order. Adjust the tension to produce smooth, even seams. A puckered seam causes the fabric to curve and distorts your piecing. Use a sharp needle in the machine to keep the fabric from snagging or distorting from thread pulls. (Dull needles usually make a popping sound as they enter the fabric.) Adjust the stitches so they hold the seams in place securely but are easy to remove if necessary.

Needles

Use sewing-machine needles for cotton fabrics (size 70/10 or 80/12). You also need hand-sewing needles (Sharps) and hand-quilting needles (Betweens #8, #9, or #10).

Thread

Use 100% cotton, cotton-wrapped polyester, or polyester sewing thread. Do not use thread especially made for hand quilting to machine piece your quilts.

Pins

You need a supply of glass- or plastic-headed pins. Long pins are especially helpful when pinning thick layers together.

Iron and Ironing Board

Press frequently and carefully to ensure a smooth, accurately stitched quilt top. Use an iron in good working order and an ironing board that is correctly positioned for your height.

Flannel Board

When working with many small pieces (or if you just want to see how a block looks before sewing it together), lay them out on a flannel board. The board transports easily to the sewing machine when you are happy with the fabric arrangement. If you do not wish to make a flannel board, a single piece of flannel or needlepunch is effective.

To make a flannel board:
1. Cut one 16" x 16" square of cardboard.
2. Cut one 18" x 18" square of needlepunch or flannel.

3. Lay the needlepunch on the cardboard. Bring the needlepunch edges around to the back side and tape in place.

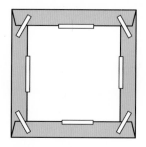

Fabric

Choosing Fabric

A good rule of thumb in selecting fabric for a quilting project is to buy the best you can afford (although the most expensive fabric is not necessarily the best).

Light to medium-weight, high quality (firmly woven) 100% cotton fabric produces the best results in any quilting project. A good quality fabric is reasonably wrinkle-free, uniform, and closely woven with long, fine threads. The dyes penetrate through to the back side. A poor quality fabric wrinkles easily when squeezed and is uneven or loosely woven with short, weak threads. The color lies on the front only.

For fabrics used in large, bed-size quilts, always wash, preshrink, and test for colorfastness. Normally, I do not prewash fabric purchased specifically to make a wall hanging since the finished project likely will not be washed. Allowing the sizing to remain in the fabric gives the hanging a crisper look. If you choose not to prewash, be sure to select fabrics that are less likely to bleed. Then accidental exposure to moisture won't damage the quilt.

Choosing Colors and Prints

Color use is a personal choice. The only person to please is you. If you are unsure how to select colors that will look nice together in a finished project, try the "blender technique."

A blender fabric is one with four or more colors. Choose a bolt of fabric you really love and use this bolt as a palette when selecting colors. The fabric company's designer has already done the work of coordinating the colors for you. If you like the tones and colors in the blender fabric and choose those tones and colors for coordinating fabrics, chances are you will be pleased with the finished project.

Lay your fabric choices on the background you've chosen, then stand back. Take off your glasses, squint, or use a Ruby Beholder™ value-finding tool to see if any of the colors blend too closely. For best results, keep each value distinct. If any of the fabrics are too close in value, try another fabric until you have the right range.

Use prints in proportion to their placement in the project. If you need just a small piece in the block, use a small print. A large piece can more successfully show off a large-scale print.

General Techniques

Rotary Cutting

1. Fold the fabric in half lengthwise, matching selvages. Place the fabric on the cutting mat so that the length of the fabric lies to the right with the raw edges on the left. (Reverse all techniques for cutting if you are left-handed.)

2. Align a Bias Square ruler with the fold and place a long ruler against it. Remove the Bias Square. Press down firmly on the ruler to keep it from moving. Place the blade next to the ruler, and, exerting an even pressure on the rotary cutter, begin cutting. Always roll the cutter away from you, never toward you. As you cut, move your fingers along the ruler as necessary to hold it steadily in place. (I call this inch worming!) After cutting, check to see if all the layers have been cut. If not, try again, applying more pressure to the cutter.

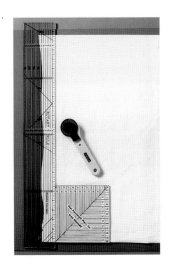

3. Place fabric to the right and measure from the left straight edge. If, for instance, you need a 2" x 44" strip of fabric, align the fabric edge along the 2" line on the ruler and cut along the ruler's edge.

4. Turn the strip horizontally and cut to the desired size.

Pressing

As a rule, quilters press seam allowances to one side, toward the darker of the fabrics. To make matching easier and to reduce bulk, I give instructions for pressing the seam allowances when it is important. Press the seam allowances in the direction of the arrows in the illustrations. If there are no pressing directions given, press seam allowances toward the darker fabric. Finger-press whenever you can, especially if you are not sure in which direction the seam allowances should lie later in the project.

When pressing with an iron, do not use steam; it distorts pieces (especially smaller ones) and can even change the shape of the block. Use a spray bottle instead. I usually set the iron on a cotton setting, but I always check the temperature when I'm working with white-on-white fabrics—they tend to scorch easily.

Place a freshly laundered, folded towel on the ironing board when pressing your blocks. The towel helps ease out any unwanted fullness, so your project lies flat.

After sewing a seam, turn the piece over. On the back side of your project, "tack press" by lightly touching the iron to the seam allowances to get them started in the right direction. On the front side, lightly spray and, with gentle pressure, press from the center out. Check that all the seams are pressed correctly on the back when finished.

Embroidery Stitches

Blanket Stitch with Appliqué

This embroidery stitch has become more popular recently due to its use with fusible appliqué. Running a row of blanket stitches around the edges of the fused appliqué pieces gives a more finished look and protects the edges from peeling up.

Choose a light- or medium-weight fusible web that a needle can penetrate. Follow the manufacturer's instructions for fusing appliqué pieces in place. To penetrate the fused fabric, use a larger needle than you normally would. Thread the needle with three strands of embroidery floss.

1. Begin by bringing the thread to the front from the back, coming out right next to the edge of the appliqué piece at A. Insert the needle through all layers at B, bring the needle out at the edge of the appliqué piece at C, and loop the thread under the tip of the needle.

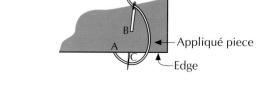

2. Pull the thread through just until snug. Be sure the stitches lie close to the edges of the appliqué but are not so tight that they pull or pucker the piece. Insert the needle at evenly spaced intervals for a uniform edge.

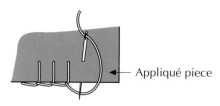

Blanket Stitch

Cross-Stitch

1. To make cross-stitches, bring the needle out of the appliqué fabric at A, about 1/8" from the edge. Make a diagonal stitch, about 3/8" long, inserting the needle into the background fabric at B. Bring the needle out again in the appliqué fabric at C. Repeat to the end of the row.

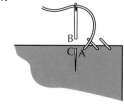

2. Insert the needle at D, right next to B as shown. Bring the needle out at E, right next to C. Repeat to the end of the row.

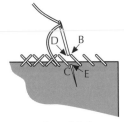

Cross-Stitch

Stem Stitch

Bring the needle out at A. Insert the needle at B and bring it out again at C. Keep the embroidery floss above the needle as you take each stitch.

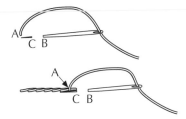

❆ Machine Piecing ❅

Accuracy is important when machine piecing. Use a $1/4$"-wide seam allowance for all the projects in this book. Achieve this width by moving the needle position so that it is $1/4$" from the right side of the presser foot, or measure $1/4$" to the right of the needle and mark the seam allowance on the sewing machine with a piece of masking tape. You can also buy a presser foot that measures $1/4$" from the needle to the outside edge.

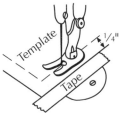

Matching Points

It is not always easy to line up seams and match points perfectly. I will tear out a point and try to fix it up to six times! After that, I recut the ripped out pieces (by then they are distorted) and try again.

I use several techniques to make perfect points.

- When matching seam lines while sewing pieces together, make sure the seam allowance on the bottom is pressed so that it moves easily over the feed dogs. Keep the top seam allowance pressed in the opposite direction. In other words, whenever possible, work with opposing seam allowances. This way the seams "lock" into position and line up exactly. Pin seam allowances in place if necessary.

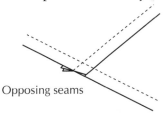

Opposing seams

- If the pieces being joined are slightly different in length, pin each piece at the seam and sew with the "big on bottom" method. The feed dogs ease the fullness of the bottom piece, pushing both pieces through the needle together.

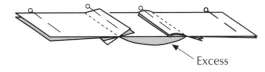

Excess

- To match points, poke a pin into one point along the seam line and through to the seam or other point where it must match. Slide the

fabric pieces together until the pin is perpendicular to the fabric and the pieces line up. Pin securely on each side of the point you are matching. Remove the first pin and stitch.

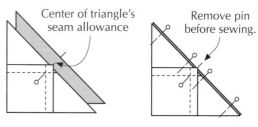

Matching points

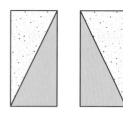

Tip

Stitch to within ¹⁄₂" to 1" of the intersection and stop with the needle down. Set the sewing machine for longer stitches, then continue stitching ¹⁄₂" to 1" past the intersection. With the needle down, reset the stitch length to the standard stitch and continue to the end of the row. When finished with the seam, check to see if the points match. If they do, restitch over the long stitches. If they do not match, remove the long stitches, adjust and repin, then repeat the procedure until the points match. I admit there are times I resort to basting by hand!

Bias Rectangles

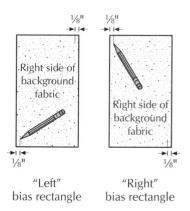

Bias rectangles

Many quilters dislike using templates and are more comfortable cutting rectangles or squares using rotary-cutting methods. The bias-rectangle method eliminates the need for templates and allows you to make small numbers of units. If you need more than ten bias-rectangle units, use Mary Hickey's technique, given in her book *Angle Antics* (That Patchwork Place), for making bias-rectangle units with the BiRangle ruler. This tool is specially designed to make multiple bias-rectangle units.

Finger-press small bias-rectangle units. Ironing distorts them.

Marking a Bias-Rectangle Unit
Cutting Rectangles

When cutting two rectangles to make a bias-rectangle unit, cut each rectangle ¹⁄₂" larger than the finished dimensions of the bias-rectangle unit. For example, for a bias-rectangle unit with finished dimensions of 1¹⁄₂" x 3", cut each rectangle 2" x 3¹⁄₂". All bias-rectangle unit measurements in this book include seam allowances.

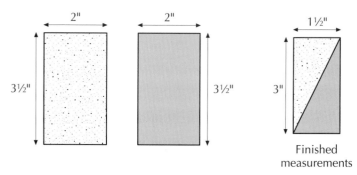

Finished measurements

Marking Rectangles

The projects in this book usually call for both "right" and "left" bias-rectangle units. These are bias-rectangle units with their diagonal seam lines running in opposite directions from each other. These two units are often joined to make roofs or treetops.

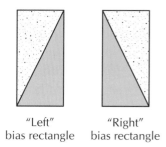

"Left" bias rectangle   "Right" bias rectangle

Be sure to mark and sew bias-rectangle units correctly. Always refer to the illustrations when in doubt. Each pattern in the book indicates how many bias-rectangle units you need and whether they are right or left bias-rectangle units.

1. Mark ¹⁄₈" from the outside edges on the right side of the background rectangle.

"Left" bias rectangle   "Right" bias rectangle

2. Mark ¹⁄₈" from the outside edges on the wrong side of the contrasting rectangle.

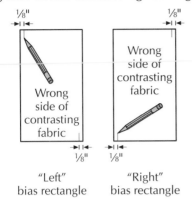

"Left" bias rectangle   "Right" bias rectangle

Note: The ¹⁄₈" markings on the wrong side of the contrasting rectangles are reversed from the markings on the right side of their corresponding background rectangles as shown.

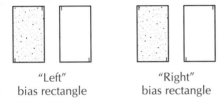

"Left" bias rectangle   "Right" bias rectangle

Note: When placing the two rectangles with right sides together, always put the background rectangle on the bottom and the contrasting rectangle on top.

3. On the wrong side of the contrasting rectangles only, draw a diagonal line from the ¹⁄₈" upper corner mark to the ¹⁄₈" lower corner mark as shown. Use a fine-point permanent-ink marker or sharp pencil to draw lines.

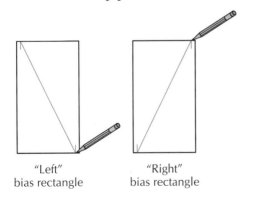

"Left" bias rectangle   "Right" bias rectangle

Sewing Bias-Rectangle Units
To make the right *bias-rectangle unit:*
1. With right sides together, lay the contrasting rectangle on top of the background rectangle. Turn the contrasting rectangle *counterclockwise* until the ¹⁄₈" mark in the upper right

corner touches the ¹⁄₈" mark on the background rectangle's upper left corner as shown. The ¹⁄₈" mark in the contrasting rectangle's lower left corner should touch the ¹⁄₈" mark of the background rectangle's lower right corner. Stitch on the line.

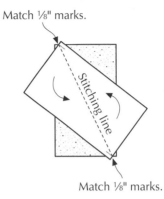

Match ¹⁄₈" marks.

Match ¹⁄₈" marks.

2. Cut away the excess fabric as shown, leaving a ¹⁄₄"-wide seam allowance. Finger-press the seam allowances toward the background rectangle.

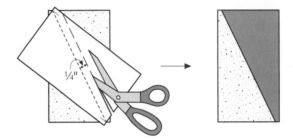

To make the left *bias-rectangle unit:*
With right sides together, lay the contrasting rectangle on top of the background rectangle. Turn the contrasting rectangle *clockwise* until the ¹⁄₈" mark in the upper left corner touches the ¹⁄₈" mark in the background rectangle's upper right corner as shown. The ¹⁄₈" mark in the contrasting rectangle's lower right corner should touch the ¹⁄₈" mark of the background rectangle's lower left corner. Stitch on the line.

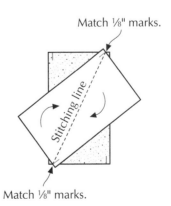

Match ¹⁄₈" marks.

Match ¹⁄₈" marks.

Angled Piecing

I have found that the following Template-Free methods of sewing angles are more accurate, less intimidating, and much easier than using templates. The method used depends upon the direction of the angle or the number of angles in each piece. When sewing angles, place the fabrics with right sides together and draw a diagonal line on the wrong side of one of the pieces. Use a fine-point permanent-ink marker or sharp pencil. Make sure to draw the line at the angle shown in the illustrations. Sew exactly on the drawn line and cut away the excess fabric, leaving a 1/4"-wide seam allowance.

To sew a small square to a larger piece:
1. Draw a diagonal line on the *wrong* side of the small square.
2. With right sides together and referring to the illustration below, lay the square on the other fabric piece where indicated in the pattern, making sure the diagonal line lies in the proper direction.

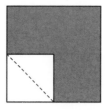

3. Stitch on the diagonal line and cut away excess fabric, leaving a 1/4"-wide seam allowance. Press seam allowances toward the dark fabric unless directed otherwise.

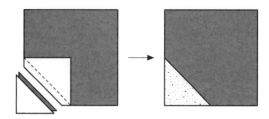

Note: When sewing two or more squares to another piece of fabric, add one square, cut away excess, and press. Then add another square, cut away, and press, repeating until you've added all the squares.

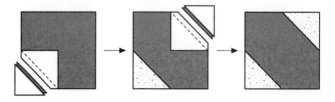

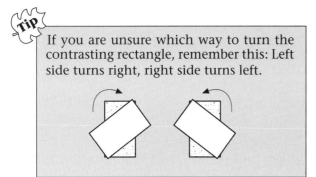

Tip

If you are unsure which way to turn the contrasting rectangle, remember this: Left side turns right, right side turns left.

4. Cut away the excess fabric along the cutting line as shown, leaving a 1/4"-wide seam allowance. Finger-press the seam allowances away from the background rectangle.

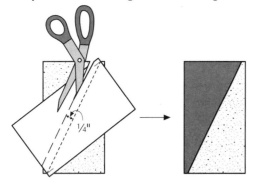

If you make more than one bias-rectangle unit, chain piece them together. To chain piece, stitch each set of rectangles without breaking the threads or lifting the presser foot between sets. Clip threads between sets when all the sets are sewn together.

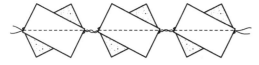

For roof or treetop units, rotate right and left bias-rectangle units 180° and then sew them together to make the unit shown.

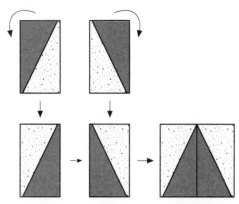

Note: Always assemble one bias-rectangle unit first, then check that it is correct before continuing with the remaining pieces.

To sew a rectangle to a rectangle:
1. With right sides together, lay a rectangle on top of another rectangle at a 90° angle, matching corners.

2. Draw a line at a 45° angle from the corner of the top rectangle to the corner of the bottom rectangle.

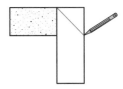

3. Stitch along the diagonal line and cut away excess fabric, leaving a ¼"-wide seam allowance. Press seam allowances toward the dark fabric unless directed otherwise.

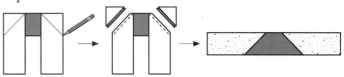

Note: For a rectangle with an angled seam at each end, sew a rectangle to each end of the center rectangle, one at a time, then cut away excess and press.

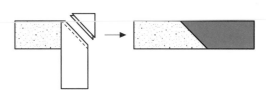

Templates for Glove Veggies
See photo on page 24.

Checker square

Finishing Your Project

Adding Borders

I often make my border choices after I complete the center of the quilt top. If, when you finish your project, you don't have fabric on hand to make borders for your quilt, take your project to a quilt shop and lay it on several different fabrics to decide what looks best. Unroll the fabric from the bolt several times and place the project on the fabric. Extend the fabric on at least two sides of the project as though the borders were in place. Step back and see what works best.

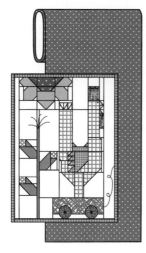

All the borders for the quilts in this book are straight cut. Cut borders to the measurements given and add them in the order indicated. If your seam allowances are an accurate $1/4$"-wide and the size of the project is correct, the measurements given will fit just fine. However, experience has shown that this doesn't always happen. I make a habit of measuring the width through the center of the quilt and cutting the top and bottom borders to match the measurements.

Note: To sew borders to the quilt evenly, mark the center of the border and the center of the quilt top at the edge before sewing. Match these points when pinning the border to the quilt. Mark or pin again between the center and edges or more frequently as desired.

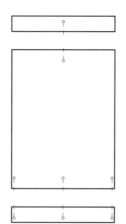

Next, measure the length through the center of the quilt, including the borders just added. Cut both side borders this length, stitch, and press.

This method squares up the project, making opposite sides the same length so that the quilt lies flat.

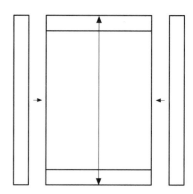

Batting and Backing

Choosing the right batting and backing for a project is just as important as the initial selection of fabric for the top. Consider durability, appearance, and the way the quilt will be cared for and cleaned.

The choices for a wall hanging will be different from those made for a bed quilt. For wall hangings, I choose a flat batting (100% cotton or a cotton blend) that will hang flat against the wall. These battings can be machine or hand quilted.

On larger projects, high-loft polyester battings give a fat, cushion look, like a comforter. These thick battings are more difficult to handle, but can be machine quilted or tied. Low-loft cotton or cotton-blend batting is perfect for hand quilting and gives a more supple, traditional look.

Selecting batting is a personal choice. Take time to try different quilting techniques on different types of batting and weights. This will give you a feel for the look you want and the degree of difficulty in handling the batting.

For backing, I usually use muslin or piece many scraps together until I have the desired size. Using scraps is a great way to use leftovers and create an interesting quilt back. Keep in mind whether you will machine or hand quilt your work. If you plan to hand quilt, choose a backing fabric that will show the beautiful hand stitches and allow a quilting needle to easily slip through.

Cut the backing 4" larger than the size of the finished top. For large quilts, there are 90"- and 108"-wide fabrics now available. If it is necessary to piece the backing to get the size needed, join two or three lengths of fabric. Press the seams open.

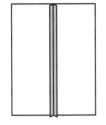 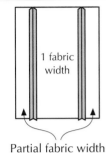

Two lengths of fabric seamed in the center

Partial fabric width

Assembling the Layers

"Sandwiching" is the term commonly used to describe joining the three quilt layers. Begin by laying the backing, wrong side up, on a flat surface. Tape the backing to the tabletop or floor with masking tape around all four edges. Do not pull tight but do smooth out all the wrinkles. Next, lay the batting on top of the backing and smooth out. Make sure it covers the entire backing. If the batting is very wrinkled, spray it lightly with water and throw the batting in the dryer for approximately five minutes. Lay the quilt top, right side up, on the batting. Smooth out wrinkles from the center to the outside.

You are now ready to baste. For smaller projects, pin-baste with rust-proof, 1"-long safety pins spaced approximately four inches apart. Work from the center out, avoiding any marked quilting lines.

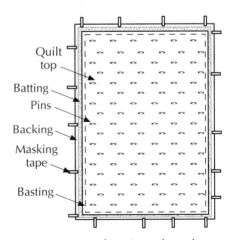

Quilt top
Batting
Pins
Backing
Masking tape
Basting

Use safety pins to baste layers together for machine quilting.

For larger projects, hand baste the layers together. Using a long needle, brightly colored thread, and large stitches, begin at the center and baste to the top outer edge. Return to the center and baste toward the bottom outer edge of the quilt. Return to the center again and baste toward one side of the quilt, then baste from the center to the opposite side. Continue returning to the center and basting out, creating a starburst effect.

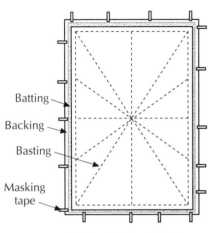

Batting
Backing
Basting
Masking tape

Basting for Hand Quilting

Quilting

Machine or hand quilt your project as desired. In the past, most quilts were quilted by hand. Today, quiltmakers have the advantage of choosing either method or a combination of both. Time is usually the deciding factor. An excellent source on hand quilting is *Loving Stitches* by Jeana Kimball; for machine quilting, refer to *Machine Quilting Made Easy* by Maurine Noble (both from That Patchwork Place).

When quilting is complete, remove the long basting stitches and trim the batting and backing to the size of the top. Now you are ready to bind and sign your quilt.

Binding

The binding requirements given for the projects in this book are adequate if your seam allowances are an accurate $1/4$" wide. Again, I urge you to measure through the center of the quilt for binding strip lengths, as you did for borders.

The following directions are for making French binding. Because of its double thickness, this binding is sturdy and wears well.

1. Cut the number of strips indicated and, if necessary, join end to end at a 45° angle. Fold in half lengthwise, wrong sides together, and press.

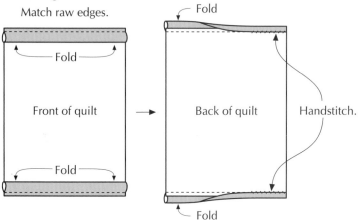

2. Measure the width of the quilt through the center and cut two strips this length.
3. On the front of the quilt, with raw edges even, stitch a strip to the top and bottom. Use a $1/4$"-wide seam allowance. After stitching, fold the binding over the seam allowance and to the back. Hand stitch to the back along the seam line.

4. Next, measure through the center from top to bottom and add 1" to this measurement. Cut two strips this length.
5. On each end, fold under $1/2$" and press (the folded-under $1/2$" gives the binding a clean, finished edge). With wrong sides together, press strips in half lengthwise and stitch the binding to the quilt, following the same procedures given in step 3.

For more ideas on finishing your quilt, refer to *Happy Endings* by Mimi Dietrich (That Patchwork Place).

Match raw edges.

Fold — Fold — Front of quilt

Fold — Fold — Back of quilt — Handstitch.

Fold

16

"Winter Evening" by
Retta Warehime, 1994,
Kennewick, Washington,
36½" x 33". In the cool of the
evening, there is no more melting
for this little snowman. Quilted by
Vi McDonald.

"Miniature Lighted Tree" by
Retta Warehime, 1994, Kennewick,
Washington, 29" x 38". The original
"Lighted Tree" quilt is 59" x 75",
therefore "miniature" was added to the
name of this version of the Colorado Log
Cabin and Steps to the Altar wall
hanging. The twinkling stars give this
"Miniature Lighted Tree" a special
holiday warmth.

"Country Stocking" by
Retta Warehime, 1994,
Kennewick, Washington,
10 1/2" x 20". Santa,
checkerboards, buttons,
and stars are the perfect
additions to any
"Country Stocking."

"Place Mats" by
Retta Warehime,
1994, Kennewick,
Washington,
17 1/4" x 11 1/4".
Join the
festivities!
Incorporate
colors and fabric
design to make
these place mats
fit perfectly into
the holiday of
your choice.
Quilting stencil by
Deer Meadow
Designs.

"Halloween Sampler" by Retta Warehime, 1993, Kennewick, Washington, 35 1/2" x 29". Pumpkins, bats, and whimsical stars make up this Halloween quilt. Quilted by Vi McDonald.

"Small Halloween Sampler" by Retta Warehime, 1993, Kennewick, Washington, 33 1/2" x 19 1/2". Make this small sampler variation using Moon, Star, Pumpkin, and Bat blocks from the "Halloween Sampler" quilt. Directions for blocks begin on page 29. Quilted by Donna Thorne.

"Midnight Meow" by Retta Warehime, 1994, Kennewick, Washington, 20 ½" x 22 ½". "Midnight Meow" is not necessarily for Halloween. Cat lovers can make this a part of their permanent decor by changing the colors. Quilted by Vi McDonald.

"Cats' Night Out" floorcloth designed by Retta Warehime. Made by Kathy Renzelman, 1994, Ashburn, Virginia, 26" x 20". You can almost hear these midnight serenaders. If you just can't step on this pair, hang them on the wall.

"Star of Wonder" designed by Retta Warehime. Made by Jackie Gest-Easton, 1994, Pasco, Washington, 60" x 75". Originally this was to be called "Blazing Poinsettias." As the piecing progressed, Jackie's husband Chuck decided it would be better to call it "Star of Wonder." Quilted by Chris Mewhinney.

"Morning Harvest" by Retta Warehime, 1994, Kennewick, Washington, 28½" x 36½".
The rooster is crowing, the sun is shining, and so grows the corn. Quilted by Vi McDonald.

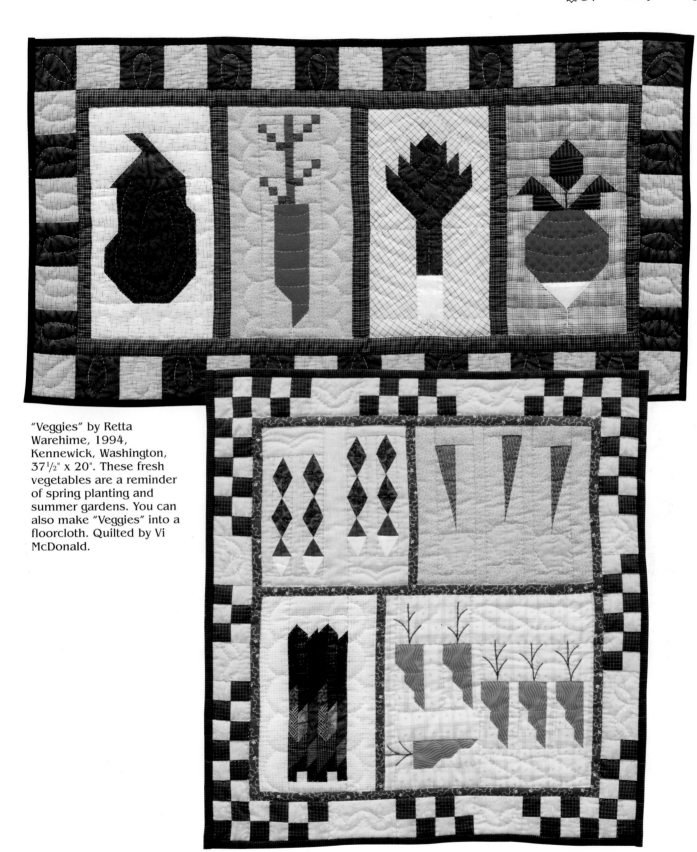

"Veggies" by Retta Warehime, 1994, Kennewick, Washington, 37½" x 20". These fresh vegetables are a reminder of spring planting and summer gardens. You can also make "Veggies" into a floorcloth. Quilted by Vi McDonald.

"Garden Fresh in Miniature" by Retta Warehime, 1994, Kennewick, Washington, 23" x 24". For all of us who love gardening, this small hanging brings the spring harvest indoors. Quilted by Vi McDonald.

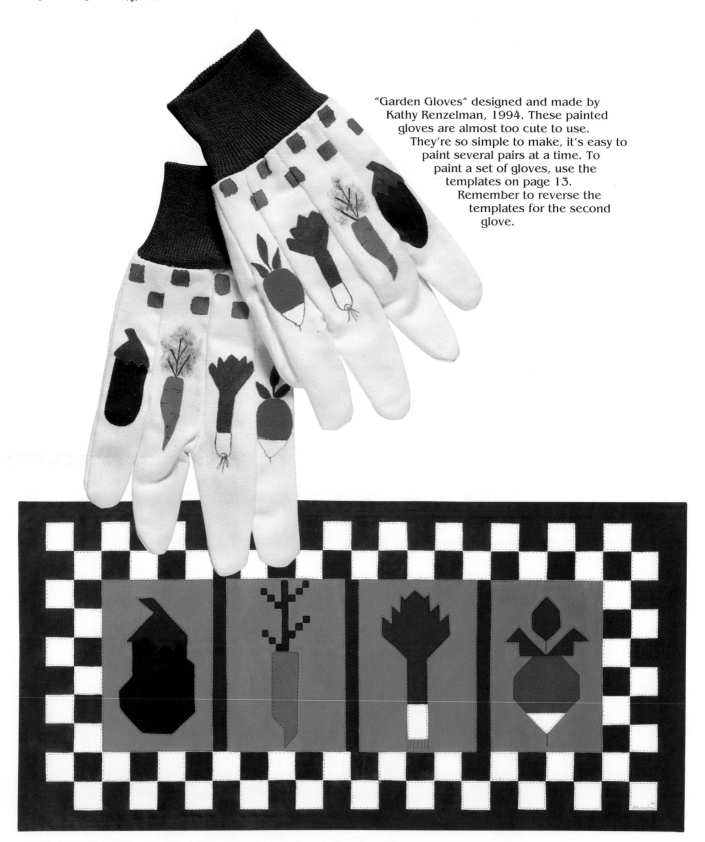

"Garden Gloves" designed and made by Kathy Renzelman, 1994. These painted gloves are almost too cute to use. They're so simple to make, it's easy to paint several pairs at a time. To paint a set of gloves, use the templates on page 13. Remember to reverse the templates for the second glove.

"Veggies from the Garden" designed by Retta Warehime. Painted by Kathy Renzelman, 1994, Ashburn, Virginia, 48" x 24". This is the perfect floorcloth for your country kitchen. Place it in front of the kitchen sink or hang it in the greenhouse.

Quilt Patterns

Country Stocking

Photo on page 18
Size: 10½" x 20"

Materials: 44"-wide fabric

⅜ yd. tan for stocking front and back
⅛ yd. white for checkerboard and Star blocks
¼ yd. red for checkerboard, heel, and toe
⅛ yd. yellow for stars

Assorted red, white, peach, and green scraps for Santa, face, beard, and tree
⅜ yd. for lining
12" x 22" rectangle of needlepunch
⅛ yd. paper-backed fusible web
7 buttons in assorted sizes and colors

Cutting					
Cut strips across the width of the fabric from selvage to selvage unless otherwise noted.					
Fabric	**No. of Strips**	**Strip Width**	**Piece**	**No. of Pieces**	**Dimensions**
Tan	1	12"		1	12" x 14"
				1	12" x 22"
White	2	1½"*		1	1½" x 44"
			C	8	1½" x 1½"
			B	4	1½" x 2½"
			E	2	1½" x 3½"
			F	1	1½" x 4½"
Red	1	1½"		1	1½" x 44"
Yellow	1	1½"	A	4	1½" x 1½"
			D	2	1½" x 3½"
Green				1	1" x 5"
Lining				2	12" x 22"
Cut B, C, E and F from one strip, reserve the second.					

Unit Assembly

Use the stocking pattern on the pullout pattern insert.

1. Trace the stocking pattern onto the 12" x 14" tan piece and cut out the stocking front.
2. Trace the heel, toe, tree, Santa, beard, face, and mustache patterns onto the paper side of the fusible web. (Remember to reverse these pieces when tracing onto the paper backing.) Do not add seam allowances. Following the manufacturer's instructions, fuse the patterns onto the appropriate fabrics and cut out the pieces. Set aside.

Checkerboard

1. Sew the 1½" x 44" red and white strips together lengthwise. Press toward the red strip.
2. Crosscut the strip unit at 1½" intervals.

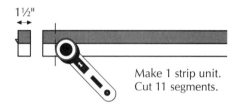

Make 1 strip unit.
Cut 11 segments.

3. Sew the units together end to end.

4. From the unit made in step 3, remove the stitching between squares to make three strips, each 7 squares long. Two strips should begin and end with red squares, and one strip should begin and end with white squares.

5. To make the checkerboard, sew a strip beginning and ending with red squares to each side of the strip beginning and ending with white squares. Press seam allowances in one direction and set aside.

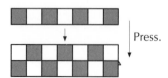

Press.

Stars

See "Angled Piecing" on pages 12–13.

1. Sew a yellow A to a white B as shown, using the angled-piecing technique. Sew a white C to the end of this unit.

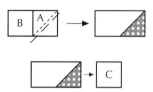

Make 4.

2. Sew a white C to each end of a yellow D, using the angled-piecing technique. Sew the angles as shown.

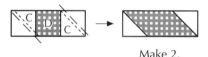

Make 2.

3. Sew a unit made in step 1 to each side of a unit made in step 2 as shown, taking care to place the units correctly.

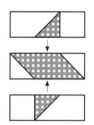

4. Sew a white E to each star unit as shown. Sew a white F to the long edge of a star unit as shown, then sew this unit to the remaining star unit.

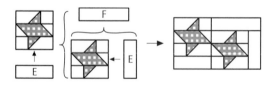

Stocking Assembly

1. Sew the checkerboard section to the star section. Sew this unit to the stocking front.

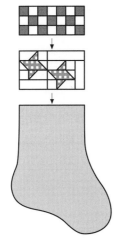

2. Following the fusible-web manufacturer's instructions, fuse the heel and toe pieces in place. Cross-stitch along the edges of the heel and toe where they join the stocking. See "Embroidery Stitches" on pages 8–9.

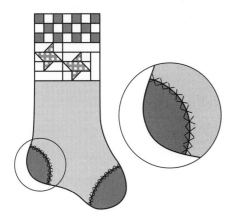

3. Place the stocking front on the 12" x 22" tan rectangle, right sides together. Trace around the stocking front, using it as a pattern to mark the stocking back. Cut out the stocking back.

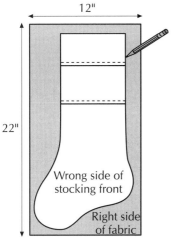

Note: If your fabrics are not placed with right sides together, the stocking front and back will face opposite directions!

4. Place the 12" x 22" rectangles of lining fabric with right sides together. Using the same pattern that you used in step 3, cut out the lining, then cut out the batting piece from the 12" x 22" rectangle of batting.

5. With right sides together, sew each set of pieces together across the top. Sew 1 lining piece to the stocking front and 1 lining piece to the stocking back.

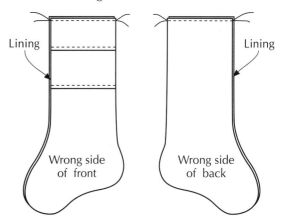

6. For the hanger, fold the 1" x 5" strip of green fabric in half lengthwise with wrong sides together; press. Open the pressed strip and fold each long edge toward the center fold. Press again. Topstitch along the edge.

7. Fold the hanging strip in half and pin to the stocking front, just below the top edge of the stocking as shown.

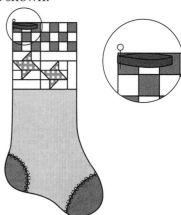

8. With right sides together, place the stocking front on top of the stocking back. Lay the batting on top of the stocking front. Pin the layers together and turn the stocking over. Using longer stitches (7 to 8 stitches per inch) sew around the stocking, leaving a 5" opening in the lining back.

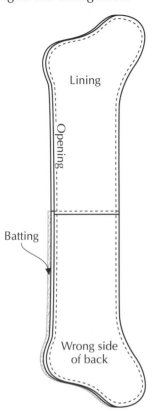

9. Clip the curves and turn the stocking right side out. Hand stitch the opening and tuck the lining into the stocking. Topstitch $1/4$" around the top of the stocking.

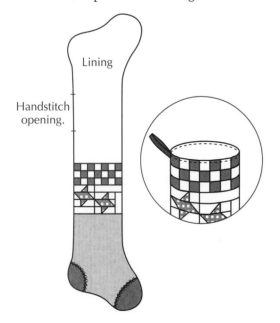

10. Following the fusible-web manufacturer's instructions, fuse the Santa and tree to the stocking front.

Finishing

Sew running-stitch lines $1/8$" inside the Santa, beard, face, and mustache, or draw stitches with a permanent-ink pen. Draw eyes on the Santa and cross-stitches along the heel and toe pieces if you have not already sewn them. Sew buttons on the tree (where Xs on the pattern indicate placement). Enjoy your Country Stocking!

Halloween Sampler

Photo on page 19
Quilt size: 35" x 28½"

Materials: 44"-wide fabric

⅞ yd. pale gold for background
⅛ yd. dark orange for moon
⅛ yd. yellow for stars
⅛ yd. blue for hat
⅛ yd. black for bat
¼ yd. medium orange for pumpkins
Scraps of green for stems

¼ yd. for accent border and sashing
½ yd. for outer border
1 yd. for backing
39½" x 33" rectangle of batting
⅓ yd. for binding
Paper-backed fusible web

Moon and Stars

Cutting					

Cut strips across the width of the fabric from selvage to selvage unless otherwise noted. Cut narrower strips from the remaining wide strips.

Fabric	No. of Strips	Strip Width	Piece	No. of Pieces	Dimensions
Gold	2	$1^1/4$"	J	28	$1^1/4$" x $1^1/4$"
			L	7	$1^1/4$" x 2"
			G	7	$1^1/4$" x $2^1/4$"
			F	1	$1^1/4$" x 6"
	1	$1^3/4$"	I	7	$1^1/4$" x $1^3/4$"
			M	1	$1^3/4$" x $2^3/4$"
			B	2	$1^1/2$" x $1^1/2$"
			C	1	$1^1/2$" x 5"
			E	2	1" x $3^1/2$"
	2	$2^1/4$"	N	4	$2^1/4$" x $2^3/4$"
			O	1	$2^1/4$" x $23^3/4$"
			P	1	2" x $23^3/4$"
	1	2"*	CC	1	2" x $3^1/2$"
			EE	1	$1^3/4$" x $4^1/4$"
			AA	1	$1^1/2$" x $3^1/2$"
			DD	1	$1^1/2$" x $4^1/4$"
			BB	1	1" x $3^1/2$"
Dark Orange	1	$2^1/2$"*	A	1	$2^1/2$" x 5"
			D	2	$1^1/2$" x $1^1/2$"
Yellow	2	$1^1/4$"	H	21	$1^1/4$" x $1^1/4$"
			K	7	$1^1/4$" x $3^1/2$"

*Cut from 22"-long strip

 Tip Use a flannel board to arrange rows (see "Flannel Board" on page 6).

Moon

See "Angled Piecing" on pages 12–13.

1. Sew a gold B to each end of a dark orange A using the angled-piecing technique. Press seam allowances toward A.

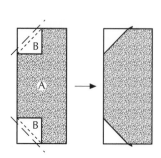

2. Sew a dark orange D to each end of a gold C, using the angled-piecing technique. Sew this unit to the unit made in step 1 as shown.

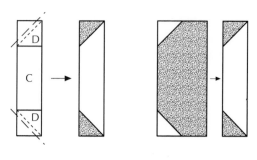

3. Sew a gold E to each end of the Moon block, then sew a gold F to the left side as shown. Press seam allowances away from the moon. The unfinished block size is $4\frac{1}{4}$" x 6".

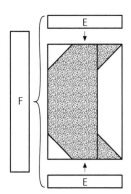

Stars

1. Sew yellow H to gold G, then sew this unit to gold I.

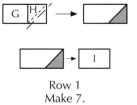

Row 1
Make 7.

2. Sew two gold J squares to yellow K.

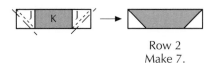

Row 2
Make 7.

3. Sew a yellow H to each end of a gold L. Sew a gold J to each end of this unit as shown.

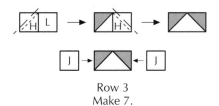

Row 3
Make 7.

4. Sew star rows 1–3 together to make a star unit. The unfinished block size is $3\frac{1}{2}$" x $2\frac{3}{4}$".

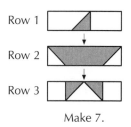

Make 7.

5. Sew a gold N rectangle between each of 5 star units, then sew a gold M to the left side.

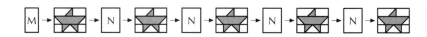

6. Sew a gold O and P to the top and bottom of the star unit, then sew the moon unit to the left side as shown to make a $27\frac{1}{2}$" x 6" section.

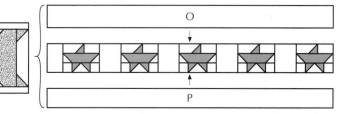

7. Sew gold AA to the top and gold BB to the bottom of one star. Sew gold CC to the top of the other star. Sew a star to each side of gold DD as shown, and sew gold EE to the right side to make an $8\frac{3}{4}$" x $4\frac{1}{4}$" section. Set aside.

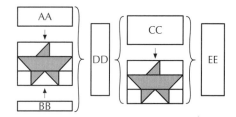

Wizard or Witch's Hat

Cutting					
Cut strips across the width of the fabric from selvage to selvage unless otherwise noted. Cut narrower strips from the remaining wide strips.					
Fabric	**No. of Strips**	**Strip Width**	**Piece**	**No. of Pieces**	**Dimensions**
Gold	1	1½"	D	5	1½" x 1½"
			L	2	1½" x 2¼"
			Q	1	1½" x 7"
			I	1	1¼" x 1¼"
			J	2	1¼" x 2¼"
			G	1	1¼" x 2½"
			N	2	1" x 1"
	1	2½"	A	1	2½" x 2½"
			F	1	2" x 2½"
			B	1	2" x 2"
			P	1	1¾" x 7"
Blue	1	2½"*	E	1	1½" x 2½"
			C	1	2½" x 3"
			M	1	2¼" x 5¾"
			O	1	1½" x 7½"
			K	1	1½" x 4¾"
			H	1	1¼" x 3¾"

*Cut from 22"-long strip.

Assembly

See "Angled Piecing" on pages 12–13.

1. Sew gold B to blue C and a gold D to each end of blue E using the angled-piecing technique. Sew these units together, then sew gold A to the left side and gold F to the right side.

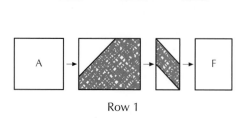

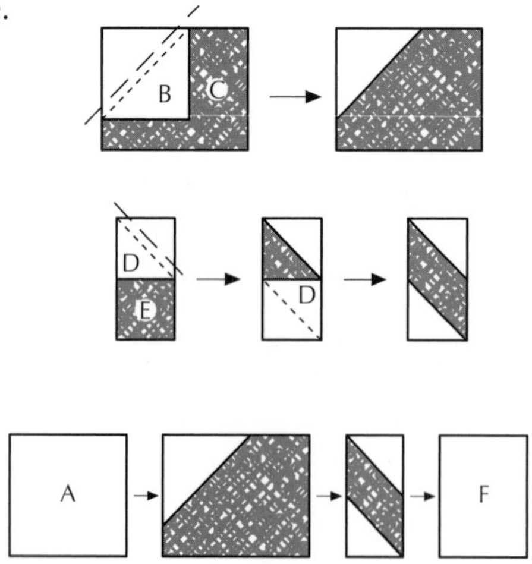

Row 1

2. Sew gold I to the right side of blue H, using the angled-piecing technique. Sew gold G to the left side and gold J to the right side.

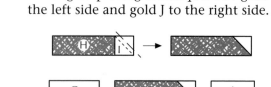

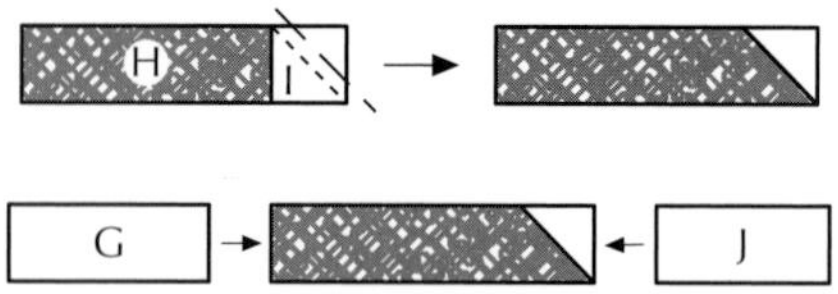

Row 2

3. Using the angled-piecing technique, sew a gold D to the left side of hat K. Sew a gold D to the left side and gold L to the right side.

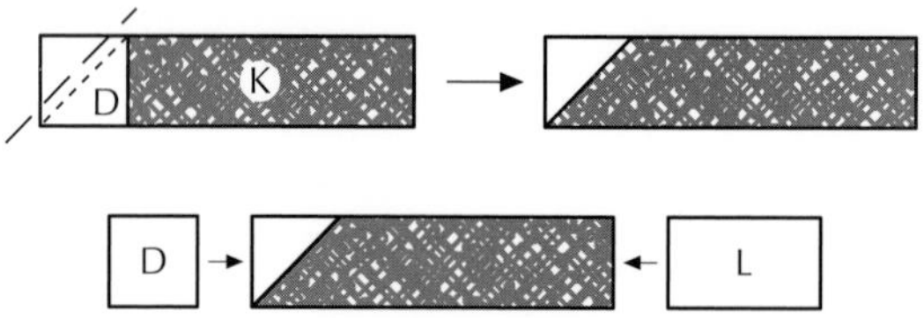

Row 3

4. Sew a gold D to blue M, using the angled-piecing technique, then sew a gold L to the left side and gold J to the right side.

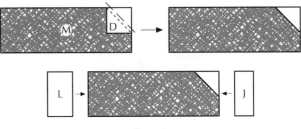

Row 4

5. Sew a gold N to each upper corner of blue O, using the angled-piecing technique.

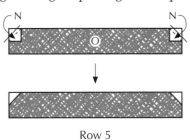

Row 5

6. Assemble rows 1–5, then sew gold P and Q rectangles to each side of the hat unit to complete the block. The unfinished block size is $7^1/_2$" x $9^3/_4$".

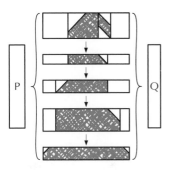

Bat

Cutting
Cut strips across the width of fabric from selvage to selvage. *Cut narrower strips from the remaining wide strips.*

Fabric	No. of Strips	Strip Width	Piece	No. of Pieces	Dimensions
Gold	2	$1^1/_2$"	I	1	$1^1/_2$" x 9"
			H	3	$1^1/_4$" x $4^1/_2$"
			A	4	$1^1/_2$" x $2^1/_2$"
			C	20	$1^1/_2$" x $1^1/_2$"
			F	8	1" x $1^1/_2$"
	1	2"	J	1	2" x 9"
			K	1	$1^1/_2$" x $8^3/_4$"
			L	1	1" x $4^1/_2$"
Black	2	$1^1/_2$"	D	4	$1^1/_2$" x $4^1/_2$"
			B	8	$1^1/_2$" x $3^1/_2$"
			G	2	$1^1/_2$" x $2^1/_2$"
			E	8	1" x $1^1/_2$"

Assembly

See "Angled Piecing" on pages 12–13.

1. For row 1, use the angled-piecing technique to sew a gold C to a black B. Then sew a gold A to the opposite end of black B. For row 7, sew a gold C and A to a black B, sewing seams in the opposite direction from row 1 as shown.

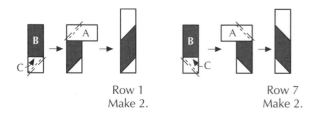

Row 1
Make 2.

Row 7
Make 2.

2. To make row 2, sew a gold C to opposite corners of a black D as shown. For row 6, sew a gold C to opposite corners of a black D, sewing seams in the opposite direction from row 2.

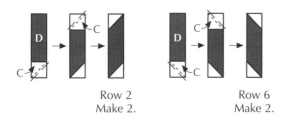

Row 2
Make 2.

Row 6
Make 2.

3. To make row 3, sew a gold C to one end of a black B. Then sew a gold C to the opposite end of black B, using the angled-piecing technique. For row 5, sew a gold C to each end of black B, paying careful attention to the seam angles.

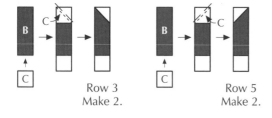

Row 3
Make 2.

Row 5
Make 2.

4. Referring to "Bias Rectangles" on pages 10–12, use black E and gold F rectangles to construct four right and four left bias-rectangle units. Join right and left bias-rectangle units, then sew a unit to each end of a black G, carefully noting the fabric and angle placement.

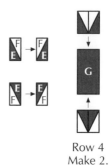

Row 4
Make 2.

5. Join rows 1–7. Arrange and sew gold strips H–J to make the $9\frac{1}{2}$" x $7\frac{1}{2}$" block. Add gold strips H, K, and L to make the $8\frac{3}{4}$" x $5\frac{1}{2}$" block as shown.

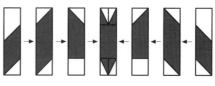

Make 2.

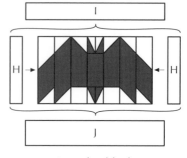

Large bat block

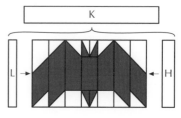

Small bat block

Large Pumpkin

Cutting					
Cut strips across the width of the fabric from selvage to selvage unless otherwise noted. Cut narrower strips from the remaining wide strips.					
Fabric	**No. of Strips**	**Strip Width**	**Piece**	**No. of Pieces**	**Dimensions**
Gold	1	2¼"*	A	1	2" x 3"
			E	1	2" x 2¾"
			F	2	1¾" x 2¼"
			B	10	1" x 1"
	1	1½"	J	2	1" x 1½"
Med. Orange	1	6½"	I	1	3¾" x 6½"
			G	1	1¾" x 5½"
			H	3	1" x 5½"
Green			C	2	1" x 1¼"
			D	1	1" x 1¾"
*Cut from 22"-long strip.					

Note: Assembly will be easier if you keep the pieces cut for each pumpkin separate.

Assembly

See "Angled Piecing" on pages 12–13.

1. Arrange green C and D pieces with 2 gold B pieces on a flannel board. Sew the stem unit together, then sew gold A to the left side and gold E to the right side.

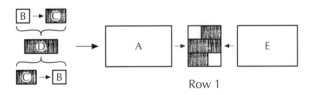

Row 1

2. Sew orange G to a gold F, using the angled-piecing technique. Sew a gold F to the opposite end as shown.

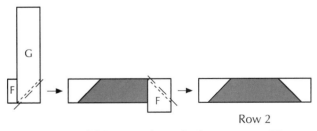

Row 2

3. Sew a gold B to each end of an orange H.

Rows 3 and 5

4. Sew a gold B to each corner of orange I, using the angled-piecing technique.

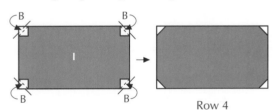

Row 4

5. Sew a gold J to each end of an orange H, using the angled-piecing technique.

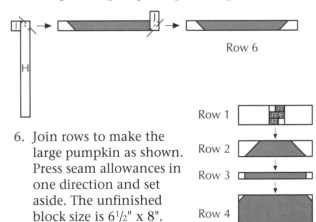

Row 6

6. Join rows to make the large pumpkin as shown. Press seam allowances in one direction and set aside. The unfinished block size is 6½" x 8".

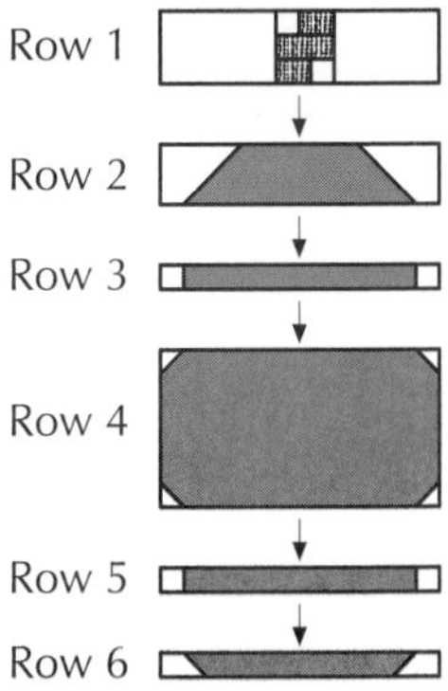

Medium Pumpkin

Cutting					
Cut strips across the width of the fabric from selvage to selvage unless otherwise noted. Cut narrower strips from the remaining wide strips.					
Fabric	No. of Strips	Strip Width	Piece	No. of Pieces	Dimensions
Gold	1	$2^3/4$"*	A	1	$2^3/4$" x $2^3/4$"
			E	1	$2^1/2$" x $2^3/4$"
			F	2	$1^1/2$" x 2"
			B	1	$1^1/2$" x $1^3/4$"
			K	2	$1^1/4$" x $1^1/4$"
			C	2	$3/4$" x 1"
			H	4	1" x 1"
Med. orange (Cut pieces from strip cut for Large Pumpkin.)					
			J	1	$4^1/4$" x $5^3/4$"
			G	1	$1^1/2$" x $4^3/4$"
			I	1	1" x $4^3/4$"
Green			D	2	1" x $1^1/4$"
*Cut from 22"-long strip.					

Assembly

See "Angled Piecing" on pages 12–13.

1. Arrange the green D pieces and the gold B and C pieces on a flannel board. Sew the stem unit together, then sew a gold A to the left side and a gold E to the right side.

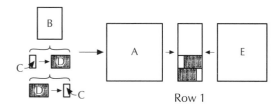

2. Sew a gold F to each end of orange G, using the angled-piecing technique.

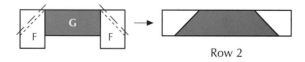

3. Sew a gold H to each end of orange I.

4. Using the angled-piecing technique, sew a gold H to each upper corner and a gold K to each lower corner of orange J.

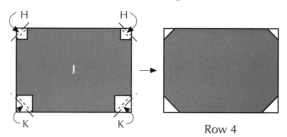

5. Join rows 1–4 to make the medium pumpkin. Press seam allowances in one direction. The unfinished block size is $5^3/4$" x 8".

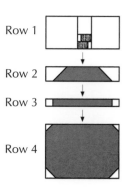

Three Small Pumpkins

Cutting					

Cut strips across the width of the fabric from selvage to selvage unless otherwise noted. Cut narrower strips from the remaining wide strips.

Fabric	No. of Strips	Strip Width	Piece	No. of Pieces	Dimensions
Gold	1	4"*	E	1	4" x 4"
			F	2	$2^{1}/_4$" x 4"
			A	6	$1^{1}/_4$" x 2"
			C	12	$1^{1}/_4$" x $1^{1}/_4$"
Med. orange			D	3	$3^{3}/_4$" x 4"
Green			B	3	1" x $1^{1}/_4$"
*Cut from 22"-long strip.					

Assembly

See "Angled Piecing" on pages 12–13.

1. Sew a gold A to each long side of each green B.

2. Sew a gold C to each corner of each orange D, using the angled-piecing technique.

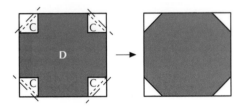

3. Sew the stem row to a long side of the pumpkin.

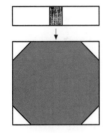

Make 3.

4. For Pumpkin 1, sew a gold E to the pumpkin unit as shown. For Pumpkins 2 and 3, sew a gold F to each remaining pumpkin unit. The unfinished block size for Pumpkin 1 is 4" x 8". The unfinished block size for Pumpkins 2 and 3 is 4" x $6^{1}/_4$".

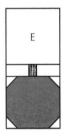

Pumpkin 1
Make 1.

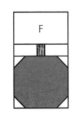

Pumpkins 2 and 3
Make 2.

Sections 4 and 5

Cutting					
Cut strips across the width of fabric from selvage to selvage.					
Fabric	**No. of Strips**	**Strip Width**	**Piece**	**No. of Pieces**	**Dimensions**
Gold	2	1½"	A	2	1¼" x 8"
			B	2	1½" x 8"
			C	1	1¼" x 6¼"
			D	1	1" x 6¼"

Assembly

1. Sew gold B strips between the large, medium, and small-pumpkin 1 blocks. Sew a gold A to each side as shown to make section 4.

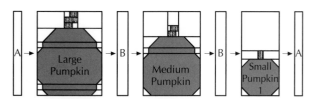

Section 4

2. Sew gold strip C between the small-pumpkin 2 and 3 blocks, then sew gold strip D to the right side to make section 5.

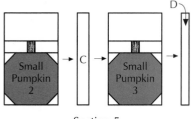

Section 5

3. Sew the small bat block to the top of pumpkin section 5.

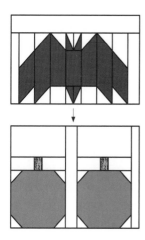

Sashing

Cutting					
Cut strips across the width of fabric from selvage to selvage unless otherwise noted.					
Fabric	**No. of Strips**	**Strip Width**	**Piece**	**No. of Pieces**	**Dimensions**
Sashing fabric	5	1"	A	3	1" x 27½"
			E	2	1" x 22"
			C	1	1" x 18¾"
			D	1	1" x 15"
			B	1	1" x 7"

Assembly

1. Sew the 2-star section to the top of the small bat block.

2. Sew sashing strip B between the hat and the large bat. Sew sashing strip B to the top of pumpkin section 4, then sew the hat and bat section to section 4.

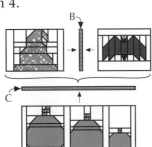

3. Sew sashing strip D between the two units made in steps 1 and 2.

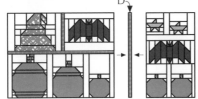

4. Sew a sashing strip A to the bottom of the moon-and-stars section, then sew this unit to the top of the section made in step 3. Sew a sashing strip A to the top and bottom of the quilt top, then sew a sashing strip E to each side.

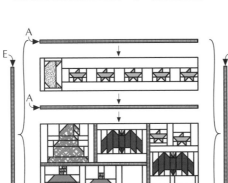

Border

1. Measure through the center of the quilt from side to side. From the accent-border fabric, cut 2 strips, each 4" wide, to this measurement. Sew a strip to the top and the bottom of the quilt.

2. Measure through the center of the quilt from top to bottom, including the borders just added. From outer-border fabric, cut 2 strips, each 4" wide, to this measurement. Sew a strip to each side of the quilt.

Finishing

1. Following the fusible-web manufacturer's directions, use the template below to cut out 3 stars from the yellow fabric. Fuse stars to the hat, referring to the quilt plan on page 29 for placement.

2. Layer the quilt top with batting and backing. Baste the layers together.

3. Quilt as desired.

4. Cut 4 strips, each 2½" x 44", from the binding fabric. Bind the quilt. (See "Binding" on page 16.)

Star
Cut 3

Midnight Meow

Photo on page 20
Quilt size: 20½" x 22½"

Materials: 44"-wide fabric

½ yd. ivory print for background
⅓ yd. black plaid #1 for cat
⅛ yd. or scraps of rust for tabs on cat
⅛ yd. or scraps of yellow print for moon
⅛ yd. orange plaid #1 for stars
⅛ yd. orange plaid #2 for accent border
¼ yd. black plaid #2 for piano key border

¼ yd. orange plaid #3 for piano key border
¼ yd. for binding
¾ yd. for backing
White embroidery floss or pearl cotton for cat's
    eyes and nose
3 strands of jute, each 6" long, for cat's whiskers
24" x 26" rectangle of batting

Cutting

Cut strips across the width of the fabric from selvage to selvage unless otherwise noted. Cut narrower strips from the remaining wide strips. "Midnight Meow" is constructed in four sections. Keep all sections separate when cutting the fabric.

Fabric	No. of Strips	Strip Width	Piece	No. of Pieces	Dimensions
Section 1					
Ivory	1	2"*	B	1	2" x 2"
			H	1	$1^7/_8$" x $1^7/_8$"
			G	2	$1^1/_2$" x $1^1/_2$"
			C	1	1" x 7"
Black plaid #1	1	$8^1/_2$"	A	1	2" x $8^1/_2$"
			F	1	$6^1/_2$" x $7^1/_2$"
			K	1	$2^1/_2$" x $5^1/_2$"
			E	1	1" x 2"
			J	1	$1^1/_2$" x $1^1/_2$"
			D	1	1" x 1"
Rust	1	$1^7/_8$"*	I	1	$1^7/_8$" x $1^7/_8$"
Section 2					
Ivory	2	$4^1/_2$"	H	1	$1^1/_2$" x 3"
			G	1	$2^1/_2$" x 3"
			I	1	3" x 9"
			A	3	$1^1/_2$" x $1^1/_2$"
			F	1	$1^1/_2$" x 5"
			B	1	1" x 1"
Black plaid #1 (Cut from section 1 black plaid strip)			C	1	$1^1/_2$" x 3"
Yellow	1	2"*	D	1	2" x 5"
			E	2	$1^1/_2$" x $1^1/_2$"
Section 3					
Ivory (Cut from section 2 ivory strip)			F	1	$4^1/_2$" x 5"
			E	1	$1^1/_2$" x $1^1/_2$"
			C	4	$1^1/_4$" x $1^1/_2$"
Black plaid #1	1	$1^1/_2$"*	D	4	$1^1/_4$" x $1^1/_2$"
			B	3	$1^1/_2$" x $4^1/_2$"
Rust (Cut from section 1 rust strip)			A	8	1" x 1"
Section 4					
Ivory	3	$3^1/_2$"	J	2	$1^1/_2$" x 17"
			H	1	2" x $3^1/_2$"
			B	8	$1^7/_8$" x $1^7/_8$"
			F	2	$1^1/_2$" x $3^1/_2$"
			A	16	$1^1/_2$" x $1^1/_2$"
			I	1	1" x 13"
			G	1	1" x $4^1/_2$"
			E	2	1" x $3^1/_2$"
Orange plaid	1	$1^7/_8$"*	C	8	$1^7/_8$" x $1^7/_8$"
			D	4	$1^1/_2$" x $1^1/_2$"

*Cut from 22"-long strip.

Note: Make a floorcloth to coordinate with "Midnight Meow." See "Cats' Night Out" on page 93.

Unit Assembly

Section 1

See "Angled Piecing" on pages 12–13.

1. Sew ivory B to black plaid A, using the angled-piecing technique.

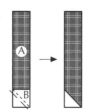

2. Sew black plaid D to ivory C, using the angled-piecing technique. Sew black plaid E to the bottom of this unit.

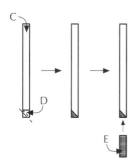

3. Sew an ivory G to the lower right corner of black plaid F, using the angled-piecing technique.

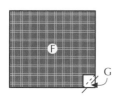

4. Draw a diagonal line on ivory H. Place this square on top of rust I, then sew ¼" on each side of the drawn line. Cut along the line and press seam allowances toward the dark fabric.

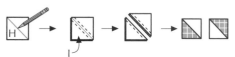

5. On a flannel board, arrange ivory G, black plaid J and K, and the units made in steps 1–5. Sew together to make section 1.

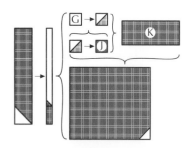

Section 1

Section 2

1. Using the angled-piecing technique, sew an ivory A to the upper left corner of black plaid C. Sew ivory B to the upper right corner of this unit.

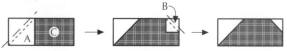

2. Using the angled-piecing technique, sew an ivory A to the upper and lower left corners of yellow D.

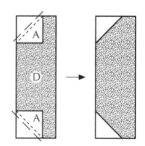

3. Using the angled-piecing technique, sew one yellow E to upper and lower left corners of ivory F.

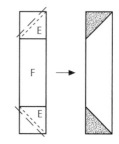

4. On a flannel board, arrange ivory rectangles G and H with the units made in steps 1–3. Join these units, then sew to ivory I.

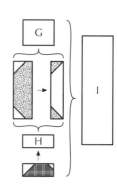

Section 2

Section 3

1. Using the angled-piecing technique, sew a rust A to 2 corners of a black plaid B as shown.

Make 2.

2. On only 1 unit made in step 1, sew a rust A to the 2 remaining corners.

Make 1.

3. Following the directions given for making bias-rectangle units on pages 10–12, make 2 left bias-rectangle units and 2 right bias-rectangle units. Use ivory C and black plaid D rectangles.

Left bias rectangle Make 2.

Right bias rectangle Make 2.

4. Sew left and right bias rectangles to each side of ivory E.

5. Join the units made in steps 1–4, then sew this unit to ivory F to make section 3.

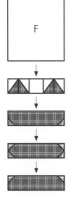

Section 3

4. Sew ivory rectangles E and F between 3 Star blocks as shown. Sew an ivory E to the top and ivory H to the bottom of the row, then sew ivory I to the right side.

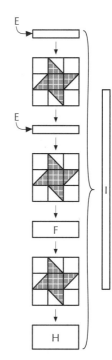

Section 4

1. Draw a diagonal line on the wrong side of ivory B. Place this square on top of an orange plaid C with right sides together and sew $1/4$" to each side of the drawn line. Cut along the line and press seam allowances toward the dark fabric. Repeat with 7 more sets of squares to make 16 half-square triangle units.

2. For each star, arrange 4 of the units made in step 1, with 1 orange plaid D and 4 ivory A squares. Sew star together.

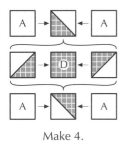

Make 4.

3. Sew 1 Star block to an ivory F, then sew ivory G to the left side of this unit.

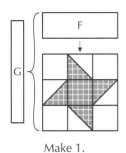

Make 1.

5. Sew the unit made in step 3 to the top of the star row made in step 4. Sew an ivory J to the left side to make section 4.

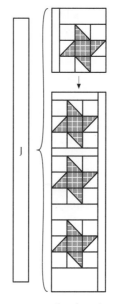

Section 4

6. Sew sections 2 and 3 together. Sew section 1 to the bottom of section 2/3. Sew section 4 to the left side. Sew the remaining ivory J to the right side of the quilt.

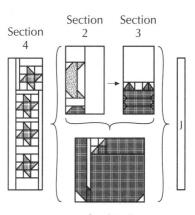

Section 1

43

Borders

Cutting				
Cut strips across the width of fabric from selvage to selvage.				
Fabric	**No. of Strips**	**Strip Width**	**No. of Pieces**	**Dimensions**
Accent Border				
Orange plaid #2	2	1¹/₂"	2	1¹/₂" x 15"
			2	1¹/₂" x 19"
Piano Key Border				
Black plaid #2	6	1"		1" x 44"
Orange plaid #3	6	1"		1" x 44"

Accent Border

1. Sew the 1¹/₂" x 15" accent-border strips to the top and bottom of the quilt. Press seam allowances toward border strips.
2. Sew one 1¹/₂" x 19" accent-border strip to each side of the quilt top. Press seam allowances toward border strips.

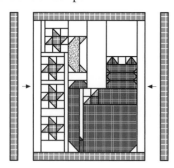

Piano Key Border

1. Sew piano-key border strips together lengthwise, alternating black and orange plaids. Press seam allowances in one direction. Crosscut at 2¹/₂" intervals to make strip-pieced rectangles.

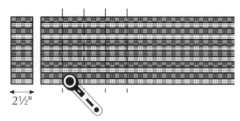

2½"

2. Sew units together end to end.

3. Count 33 keys for the top border, beginning with a dark key. Remove stitching and repeat for the bottom border. Sew borders to the top and bottom of the quilt.

4. Count 43 keys for each side border, beginning with a light key. Sew a border to each side of the quilt

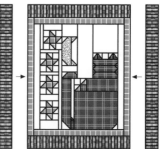

5. Sew around the outside edge with a basting stitch. Be careful not to stretch the keys.

Finishing

1. For the cat, use white embroidery floss to stitch a large X for each eye and an inverted triangle for the nose. Attach jute whiskers under the nose. Thread the strands through a large-eyed needle, take 1 stitch, and pull 3 ends through the fabric to make 3"-long whiskers. Put a dab of glue on the spot where the whiskers lie under the fabric.

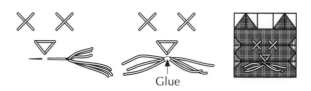

Glue

2. Layer the quilt with batting and backing. Baste the layers together.
3. Quilt as desired.
4. Cut 2 strips, each 2¹/₂" x 44", from the binding fabric. Bind the quilt. (See "Binding" on page 16.)

Miniature Lighted Tree

Photo on page 17
Quilt size: 29" x 38"
Unfinished block size: 4¼" x 5¾"

Materials: 44"-wide fabric

¾ yd. ivory print for background
⅜ yd. yellow print for stars
⅛ yd. each (or scraps) of:
    3 dark greens
    3 light greens
    red solid
    medium brown

¼ yd. red plaid for accent border
⅜ yd. dark green print for outer border
1 yd. for backing
⅜ yd. for binding
Permanent-ink marking pen
Resealable plastic sandwich bags

Block-Center Construction for Blocks 1, 2, and 6

1. From ivory fabric, cut 2 strips, each 1¼" x 44". Cut across the width of the fabric, from selvage to selvage.
2. From the red solid, cut 1 strip, 1¼" x 44".
3. To make a strip-pieced unit, sew an ivory strip to each side of the red strip.

4. Cut across the strip-pieced unit at 1¼" intervals to make 22 strip-pieced rectangles.
5. Place rectangles in a sandwich bag labeled "Blocks 1, 2, and 6." Set aside.

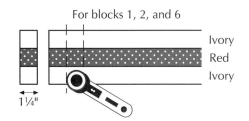

Block-Center Construction for Blocks 3, 4, and 5

Cutting				
Cut strips across the width of the fabric from selvage to selvage.				
Fabric	**No. of Strips**	**Dimensions**	**No. of Pieces**	**Dimensions**
Ivory	1	1¼" x 15"	1	1¼" x 9"
			1	1¼" x 4"
Red solid	1	1¼" x 22"	2	1¼" x 9"
			1	1¼" x 4"
A dark green	1	1¼" x 22"	2	1¼" x 9"
A light green			1	1¼" x 9"
Brown			1	1¼" x 4"

Assembly

1. For Block 3, join one ivory, red, and dark green 1¼" x 9" strip in the order shown below. For Block 4, join one dark green, red, and light green 1¼" x 9" strip in the order shown below. Press seam allowances away from the center strips. Cut across each strip-pieced unit at 1¼" intervals to make 6 strip-pieced rectangles per unit.

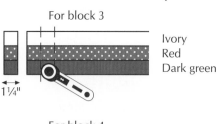

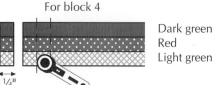

2. Sew ivory, red, and brown 1¼" x 4" strips lengthwise to make a strip-pieced unit in the order shown below. Press seam allowances away from the center strip. Crosscut at 1¼" intervals to make 2 strip-pieced rectangles.

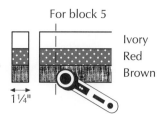

3. Place rectangles in sandwich bags labeled "Block 3," "Block 4," and "Block 5." Set aside.

Outer Block Strips

Cut the following pieces from 44"-long strips and set aside in sandwich bags marked with each color's letter (for example, "Ivory B" or "Yellow X").

Cutting					
Cut strips across the width of the fabric from selvage to selvage.					
Fabric	No. of Strips	Strip Width	Piece	No. of Pieces	Dimensions
Ivory	18	1¼"	B	104	1¼" x 2¾"
			C	64	1¼" x 4¼"
			D	22	1¼" x 3¾"
			E	12	1¼" x 3¼"
			F	6	1¼" x 2¼"
Yellow	8	1¼"	X	60	1¼" x 2½"
			Y	60	1¼" x 2¼"
Brown	1	1¼"	B	4	1¼" x 2¾"
			C	2	1¼" x 4¼"
			D	2	1¼" x 3¾"

From each of the 3 dark green fabrics, cut 1 strip, 1¼" wide. Crosscut each strip into the following pieces:

	Piece	No. of Pieces	Dimensions
Dark greens	B	8	1¼" x 2¾"
	E	4	1¼" x 3¼"
	F	4	1¼" x 2¼"

From each of the 3 light green fabrics, cut 1 strip, 1¼" wide. Crosscut each strip into the following pieces:

	Piece	No. of Pieces	Dimensions
Light greens	B	4	1¼" x 2¾"
	E	2	1¼" x 3¼"
	F	2	1¼" x 2¼"

Star Unit Assembly

Refer to "Angled Piecing" on pages 12–13 to make the following strips. Place the pieces just as the illustrations indicate. (Star units with pieces D and E have mirror images.) Be sure to sew the correct angles.

Note: For each of the star units made in steps 1–3, label a sandwich bag with the star piece's letter, and the letter and color of the piece sewn to the star piece. (All star pieces are either X or Y.) For example, label units made with ivory pieces E and yellow star pieces Y "Ivory EY." Label units made with dark green piece E and yellow star piece X "Dark green EX."

1. Sew a yellow X to each ivory and brown piece D. Sew a yellow Y to each ivory piece E.

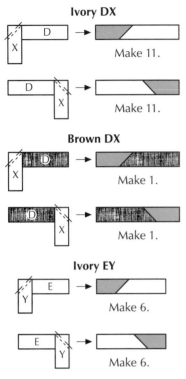

Ivory DX

Make 11.

Make 11.

Brown DX

Make 1.

Make 1.

Ivory EY

Make 6.

Make 6.

2. Sew a yellow X to each end of each dark and light green E.

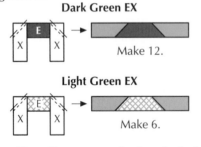

Dark Green EX

Make 12.

Light Green EX

Make 6.

3. Sew a yellow Y to one end of each dark green, light green, and ivory F rectangle. Cut away the extra, press the seam allowance open, then sew a Y to the opposite end as shown. (Don't panic! There will not be a $1/4$"-wide seam allowance at the point. Illustrations show *finished* unit.)

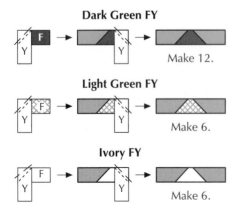

Dark Green FY

Make 12.

Light Green FY

Make 6.

Ivory FY

Make 6.

Block Assembly

Using the Courthouse Steps style of piecing, make the blocks in the order shown. Start with a strip-pieced rectangle for the block you need. (See "Block-Center Construction" on page 46). Press all seam allowances away from the center.

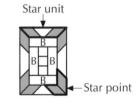

Start here.   Step 1   Step 2   Step 3   Step 4

Courthouse Steps Piecing Diagram

Assemble the blocks, following the piecing diagrams for the individual blocks. Refer to the cutting chart on page 47 for the cut dimensions of each piece B or C. Use the star-unit pieces (they have 2 letters) that you made in steps 1–3 at left. *Two star units sewn to adjacent corners of the block make one star point.*

Star unit

Star point

Block with 4 star points

Block 1

Block 1 has no star points. All pieces except the red center square are cut from ivory fabric.

Block 1
Make 12.

Block 2 and Block 2 Reversed

1. Block 2 and Block 2 reversed each have one star point. The remaining pieces are ivory except the center red square. Follow the piecing order given for pieces 1–6 in the Courthouse Steps piecing diagram above. To add star points, sew the ivory DX star unit to the block as shown, noting the position of the star fabric for Block 2 and Block 2 reversed. Stop sewing $1/4$" from the lower edge of the block and backstitch. The star unit should extend $3/4$" beyond the block. Make sure the angle of the star piece matches the angle shown in the diagram. (For Block 2 reversed, sew star units to the opposite side of the block.)

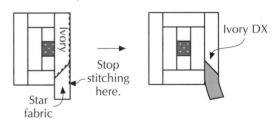

Ivory

Stop stitching here.

Star fabric

Ivory DX

Note: If you sew with the block on top of the star unit being added, you can see exactly where you need to start and stop sewing.

2. Add the adjacent star unit (ivory EY), beginning at the bottom left of the block and stopping ¼" from the block edge. Be careful not to catch any of the first star unit in the seam.

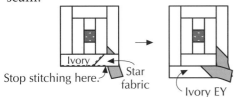

Stop stitching here. Ivory · Star fabric · Ivory EY

3. Fold the block, lining up the star units' edges as shown. Draw a line from point A to point B. To make a mitered corner, insert the needle at point A and sew along the drawn line to point B. Backstitch to secure. Cut away the excess fabric, leaving a ¼"-wide seam allowance.

A · B

4. Press the seam allowance on the star point to one side. Later, when joining the blocks, flip the direction of this seam allowance if necessary. Seam allowances lying in opposite directions on adjacent blocks make it easier to match star points. One star point will be wider than the other.

5. Sew piece C across the top of the block.

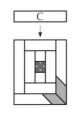

C

Block 2
Make 3.

Block 2 reversed
Make 3.

Block 3 and Block 3 Reversed

1. Block 3 and Block 3 reversed each have 3 star points. Sew pieces 1–5 to the block, following the piecing order on page 48 for Block 1. Sew ivory DX, then ivory EY to the block, stopping the stitching line ¼" from the block edge as shown.

Ivory EY · Ivory DX · Stop stitching here.

2. Pin the dark green FY and dark green EX star units to the block, matching the centers of the unit and the block and pinning to each end. Stitch, stopping ¼" from each block edge. Backstitch.

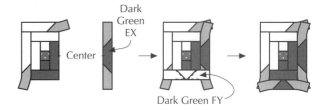

Dark Green EX · Center · Dark Green FY

Remember, if you place the block on top of the star unit, you can see exactly where you need to start and stop sewing.

Wrong side of block · Begin and end stitching

Block 3
Make 3.

Block 3 reversed
Make 3.

Block 4 and Block 4 Reversed

Make Block 4 and Block 4 reversed. Each block has 4 star points. If necessary, refer to illustrations for Block 3 and Block 3 reversed for adding star points.

Block 4
Make 3.

Block 4 reversed
Make 3.

Block 5 and Block 5 Reversed

Make Block 5 and Block 5 reversed. Each block has 2 star points.

Block 5
Make 1.

Block 5 reversed
Make 1.

Block 6

Make Block 6 with 2 star points.

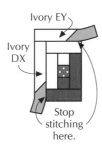

Block 6
Make 4.

Quilt Top Assembly

1. Arrange the blocks, following the layout diagram. (Refer to the photo on page 17.)

2. Sew the blocks together in horizontal rows, pressing the seam allowances for each row in opposite directions, as indicated by the arrows. Join the rows.

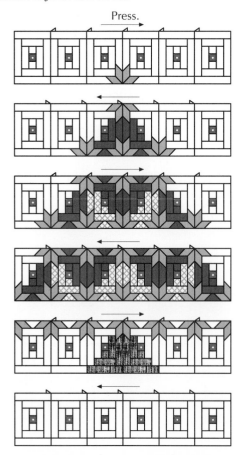

Borders

1. From the red plaid, cut 4 strips, each 1$\frac{1}{4}$" wide. Cut 2 of these strips 23" long. Sew one strip to the top and one strip to the bottom of the quilt.
2. Cut the remaining strips 33$\frac{1}{2}$" long. Sew a strip to each side of the quilt.
3. From the dark green print, cut 4 strips, each 3" wide. Cut 2 strips 24$\frac{1}{2}$" long. Sew one strip to the top and one strip to the bottom of the quilt.
4. Cut the remaining strips 38$\frac{1}{2}$" long. Sew a strip to each side of the quilt.

Finishing

1. Layer the quilt with batting and backing. Baste the layers together.
2. Quilt as desired.
3. Cut 4 strips, each 2$\frac{1}{2}$" x 44", from the binding fabric. Bind the quilt. (See "Binding" on page 16.)

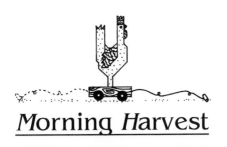

Morning Harvest

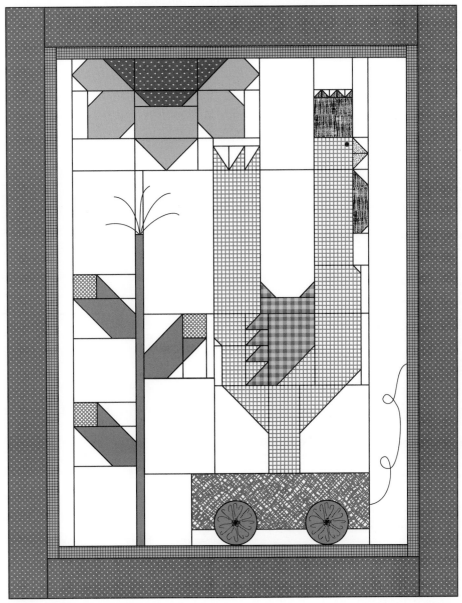

Photo on page 22
Quilt size: 29" x 37"

Materials: 44"-wide fabric

1 yd. white print for background
1/8 yd. yellow print for sun rays
1/8 yd. blue-and-yellow print for sun center
1/3 yd. gold print for rooster
1/8 yd. red print #1 for comb and wattle
Assorted scraps for beak, corn, and wheels
1/8 yd. red-and-tan plaid for wing

1/8 yd. green for corn stalk and husks
4" x 12" blue print rectangle for wagon
1/4 yd. dark red plaid for accent border
3/8 yd. green print for outer border
1/3 yd. red print #2 for binding
1 yd. for backing
1 skein each of gold and black embroidery floss

Section I

Fabric	No. of Strips	Strip Width	Piece	No. of Pieces	Dimensions
White	1	1½"	H	2	1½" x 3½"
			N	1	1½" x 2½"
			J	3	1½" x 2"
			A	8	1½" x 1½"
	1	2½"*	M	1	2½" x 4½"*
			I	2	2½" x 2½"
			L	1	1" x 3½"
Yellow	1	3½"	E	2	3½" x 3½"
			B	4	2½" x 4½"
			F	2	1½" x 1½"
Blue-and-yellow print	1	2½"*	D	1	2½" x 4½"
			C	2	2½" x 2½"
			G	1	1½" x 4½"
Gold			K	3	1½" x 2"

Cutting

Cut strips across the width of the fabric from selvage to selvage unless otherwise noted. Cut narrower strips from the remaining wide strips.

*Cut from 22"-long strip.

Assembly

See "Angled Piecing" on pages 12–13.

Row 1

1. Sew a white A to a corner of a yellow B, using the angled-piecing technique. Sew a white A to an adjacent corner of yellow B as shown.

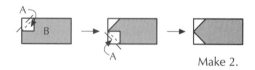

Make 2.

2. Sew a blue-and-yellow C to the end of each unit made in step 1, taking care to angle the seam correctly. Sew each unit to blue-and-yellow D to make row 1.

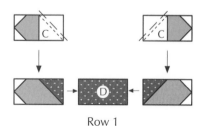

Row 1

Row 2

1. Sew a white A to 2 opposite corners of a yellow E, using the angled-piecing technique.

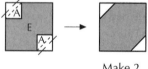

Make 2.

2. Sew a yellow F to each end of blue-and-yellow G, using the angled-piecing technique.

3. Sew a yellow B to the unit made in step 2. Sew a unit made in step 1 to each side, making sure rays are angled correctly. Sew a white H to each end to make row 2.

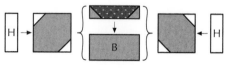

Row 2

Row 3

1. Using the angled-piecing technique, sew a white I to each end of a yellow B.

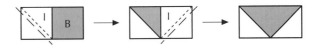

2. Using the bias-rectangle technique on pages 10–12, sew white J rectangles to gold K rectangles. Make 1 right bias rectangle and 2 left bias rectangles. Finger-press the bias-rectangle seams so you can re-press if necessary when sewing to other pieces.

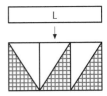

Right bias rectangle · Left bias rectangles

3. Join the bias rectangles. Sew this unit to white L.

4. Sew white M to the left side of the unit made in step 1. Sew white N to the left side of the tail-feather section. Join these units to make row 3.

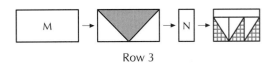

Row 3

5. Join rows 1, 2, and 3 to make section 1. Press and set aside. The unfinished section size is 12½" x 5½".

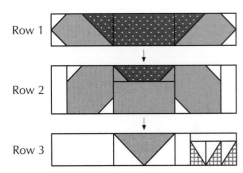

Row 1

Row 2

Row 3

Section 2

Cutting					
Fabric	**No. of Strips**	**Strip Width**	**Piece**	**No. of Pieces**	**Dimensions**
White	1	4"	I	1	4" x 7$\frac{1}{2}$"
			C	1	2$\frac{1}{2}$" x 3"
			F	1	1$\frac{7}{8}$" x 1$\frac{7}{8}$"
			A	3	1$\frac{3}{8}$" x 1$\frac{3}{8}$"
			E	1	1$\frac{1}{2}$" x 5$\frac{1}{2}$"
Red print #1	1	3"*	D	1	3" x 3"
			B	3	1$\frac{3}{8}$" x 1$\frac{3}{8}$"
Gold			H	1	2$\frac{1}{2}$" x 3"
Scrap for beak			G	1	1$\frac{7}{8}$" x 1$\frac{7}{8}$"

*Cut from 22"-long strip.

Assembly

1. Draw a diagonal line on the wrong side of a white A. Place on top of a red B, right sides together. Sew $\frac{1}{4}$" from the drawn line on each side. Cut along the line to make 2 half-square triangle units. Make 6 half-square triangle units, each 1" x 1"; you will need 5 for the comb.

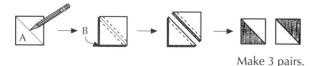

Make 3 pairs.

2. Join 5 half-square triangle units to make a 1" x 3" section. Sew white C to the top of the comb unit and red D to the bottom. Sew white E to the right side.

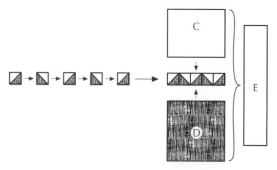

3. Draw a diagonal line on the wrong side of white F. Place on top of scrap fabric G, right sides together. Sew $\frac{1}{4}$" from the drawn line on each side. Cut along the drawn line to make two half-square triangle units. Join the units as shown.

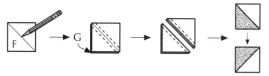

4. Sew the beak unit to gold H. Sew this unit to the comb section made in steps 1 and 2. Sew white I to the left side of the rooster unit to make section 2.

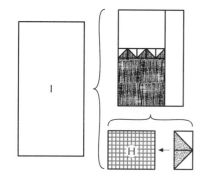

5. Sew section 1 to section 2.

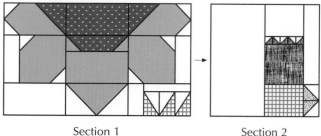

Section 1   Section 2

Section 3

Cutting

Cut strips across the width of the fabric from selvage to selvage unless otherwise noted. Cut narrower strips from the remaining wide strips.

Fabric	No. of Strips	Strip Width	Piece	No. of Pieces	Dimensions
White	1	4"	I	1	4" x 8½"
			W	1	4" x 6"
			D	1	1½" x 2½"
			A	2	1½" x 1½"
			G	1	1" x 3½"
			C	3	1" x 1"
			V	1	1" x 5"
			M	1	1" x 3"
	1	Rectangle	X	1	5" x 6"
Gold	2	3½"	K	1	3½" x 9½"
			U	1	3½" x 5"
			F	3	3½" x 3½"
			E	1	3" x 6½"
			S	1	3" x 3"
			L	1	2½" x 2½"
			Y	1	2½" x 6"
			N	1	2" x 3"
			Q	1	2" x 2"
			O	3	1½" x 1½"
Red-and-tan plaid	1	2"*	R	1	2" x 2"
			J	1	1½" x 4"
			P	3	1½" x 2"
			H	2	1½" x 1½"
	1	Rectangle	T	1	3½" x 5"
Red print #1			B	1	1½" x 4½"

*Cut from 22"-long strip.

Assembly

See "Angled Piecing" on pages 12–13.

Wattle

1. Using the angled-piecing technique, sew a white A to one end of red B. Sew a white C to the opposite end; note angle shown in illustration.

2. Sew white D to the wattle unit. Sew gold E to the left side.

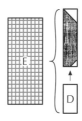

3. Sew a white C to one corner of a gold F, using the angled-piecing technique. Sew white G to the right side of this unit.

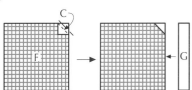

4. Sew the wattle unit to the top of the unit made in step 3.

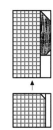

Wing

1. Sew a plaid H to the corners on one end of white I, using the angled-piecing technique. Sew plaid J to the bottom of this unit; sew gold K to the left side as shown.

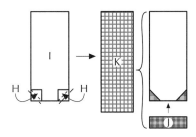

2. Sew the wing and wattle units together.

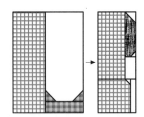

Rooster and Lower Wing

1. Using the angled-piecing technique, sew a white C to gold L. Sew white M to gold N, then sew to the bottom of the angle-pieced unit.

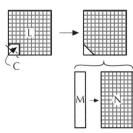

2. Using the angled-piecing technique, sew a gold O to each plaid P, and gold Q to plaid R.

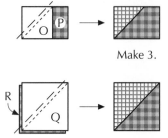

Make 3.

3. Assemble the four units made in step 2.

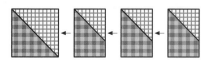

4. Using the angled-piecing technique, sew gold S to plaid T; sew white A to gold U.

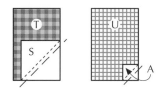

5. Join the units made in steps 1–4, then sew a white V to the right side as shown.

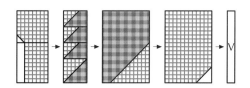

6. Using the angled-piecing technique, sew a gold F to white W and X. Sew one of these units to each side of gold Y, taking care to place the rectangles correctly.

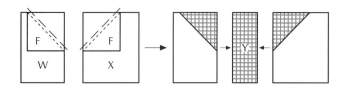

7. Join wing and rooster units, then sew to the wattle unit.

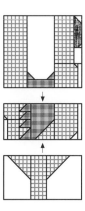

Section 4

Cutting					
Cut strips across the width of the fabric from selvage to selvage.					
Cut narrower strips from the remaining wide strips.					
Fabric	No. of Strips	Strip Width	Piece	No. of Pieces	Dimensions
White	2	1½"	Q	1	1½" x 31"
			O	1	1½" x 12"
			D	3	1½" x 1½"
	2	3"	R	1	3" x 31"
			F	3	3" x 3"
			B	3	2" x 3"
	1	4½"	J	1	4½" x 7"
			L	1	4½" x 5½"
			K	1	4½" x 4½"
			G	2	1" x 4½"
	1	5"	H	1	5" x 9½"
			I	1	5" x 6½"
			P	1	3½" x 5"
Green	1	3"	E	3	3" x 4½"
			A	3	2" x 2"
			M	1	1" x 20"
Scrap for corn			C	3	2" x 2"
Blue			N	1	4" x 12"

Assembly

See "Angled Piecing" on pages 12–13.

1. Using the angled-piecing technique, sew a green A to a white B. Sew a yellow C to the green end to make unit A.

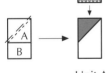

Unit A
Make 3.

2. Using the angled-piecing technique, sew a white D to one corner of a green E and a white F to the opposite corner to make unit B.

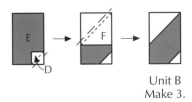

Unit B
Make 3.

3. Join units A and B to make the corn ear. Make 3 and set 2 aside for section 5.

Make 3.

4. Sew white G to the right side of the corn-ear unit, taking care that the corn points in the correct direction. Sew white H to the top of this unit and white I to the bottom to make section 4.

5. Sew section 4 to section 3.

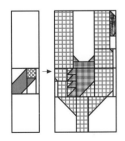

Section 4   Section 3

Sections 5 and 6

1. Sew white K between two corn ears made in step 3 of section 4. Take care that the corn points in the correct direction. Sew white J to the top of this unit and white L to the bottom.

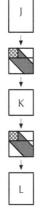

2. Sew a white G to the top of green M. Sew this cornstalk unit to the right side of the corn-ear unit made in step 1.

3. Sew white O to blue N, then sew white P to the left end of the unit.

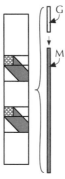

Section 5

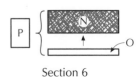

Section 6

Quilt Top Assembly

1. Join the sections as shown. Sew white Q to the left side of the quilt and white R to the right side.

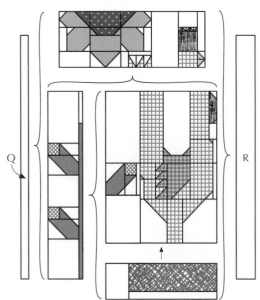

2. From scrap fabric, cut two wheels using the template on the pullout pattern insert. To make two giant yo-yos, fold the circle edges over ¼" to the wrong side and sew a row of small running stitches. (Use quilting thread for strength.) When you reach the beginning of the stitching line, pull the thread and draw the circle to the center. Tie the threads. Hand tack the wheels to the wagon.

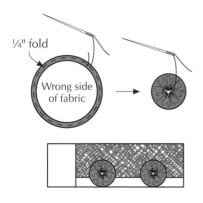

3. From red plaid, cut 4 strips, each 1¼" wide. Cut 2 strips 23" long. Sew one strip to the top and one strip to the bottom of the quilt.
4. Cut the remaining strips 32½" long. Sew a strip to each side of the quilt.
5. From green print, cut 4 strips, each 3" wide. Cut 2 strips 24½" long. Sew one strip to the top and one strip to the bottom of the quilt.
6. Cut the remaining strips 37½" long. Sew a strip to each side of the quilt.

Finishing

1. Using the stem stitch, embroider the tassels and wagon pull. (See "Embroidery Stitches" on pages 8–9.) For the tassel, embroider 5 lines with 1 row of gold next to 1 row of black. For the wagon pull, embroider a looped line with black floss. Refer to the quilt plan on page 51 for embroidery details.
2. Layer the quilt with batting and backing. Baste the layers together.
3. Quilt as desired.
4. Cut 4 strips, each 2½" x 44", from red print #2. Bind the quilt. (See "Binding" on page 16.)

Place Mats

Photo on page 18
Size: 17½" x 11½"

Materials: 44"-wide fabric

Note: Materials are enough for two place mats.

³/₄ yd. ivory for background and backing
¼ yd. white for patchwork
⅛ yd. red for patchwork

⅛ yd. yellow print for star
³/₈ yd. for binding
½ yd. needlepunch

Cutting

Cut strips across the width of the fabric from selvage to selvage.
Cut narrower strips from the remaining wide strips.

Fabric	No. of Strips	Strip Width	No. of Pieces	Dimensions
Ivory	1	13$\frac{1}{2}$"	2	13$\frac{1}{2}$" x 19$\frac{1}{2}$"
	1	9$\frac{1}{2}$"	2	9$\frac{1}{2}$" x 11$\frac{1}{2}$"
White (Crosscut only 2 of the strips)				
	4	1$\frac{1}{2}$"	30	1$\frac{1}{2}$" x 1$\frac{1}{2}$"
			12	1$\frac{1}{2}$" x 2$\frac{1}{2}$"
Red	2	1$\frac{1}{2}$"	2	1$\frac{1}{2}$" x 44"
	4 squares (cut from scraps)			1$\frac{1}{2}$" x 1$\frac{1}{2}$"
Yellow	1	1$\frac{1}{2}$"	12	1$\frac{1}{2}$" x 1$\frac{1}{2}$"
			6	1$\frac{1}{2}$" x 3$\frac{1}{2}$"
Binding fabric	4	2$\frac{1}{2}$"	4	2$\frac{1}{2}$" x 17$\frac{1}{2}$"
			4	2$\frac{1}{2}$" x 12"
Needlepunch			2	13$\frac{1}{2}$" x 19$\frac{1}{2}$"

Note: If you wish to eliminate the star and inside checker strip, cut the background piece 15$\frac{1}{2}$" x 9$\frac{1}{2}$". Make only 2 strips of 9 squares each instead of 3.

Unit Assembly

1. Join 2 red and 2 white 1$\frac{1}{2}$" x 44" strips lengthwise, alternating colors. Press seam allowances in one direction.

Press.

2. Crosscut at 1$\frac{1}{2}$" intervals to make strip-pieced rectangles. You need 56 rectangles (28 for each place mat).

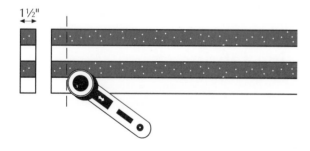

3. Join 2 strip-pieced rectangles end to end, beginning with a white square and adding a 1$\frac{1}{2}$" white square to the opposite end. Make 3 strips for each place mat.

4. Join 4 strip-pieced rectangles end to end, alternating colors. Begin with a red square and add a 1$\frac{1}{2}$" red square to the opposite end. Make 2 strips for each place mat. Press all seam allowances in one direction.

Stars

See "Angled Piecing" on pages 12–13.

1. Using the angled-piecing technique, sew a 1½" yellow square to a 1½" x 2½" white rectangle.

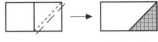

Make 12.

2. Sew a 1½" white square to the right side of the unit made in step 1. Use this unit for rows 1 and 3 of the Star block.

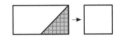

Rows 1 and 3
Make 12.

3. Using the angled-piecing technique, sew a 1½" white square to each end of a 1½" x 3½" yellow rectangle. Sew the angles in the same direction. Use this unit for row 2 of the Star block.

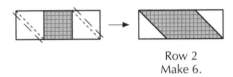

Row 2
Make 6.

4. Join rows 1, 2, and 3 to make the 3½" x 3½" Star block.

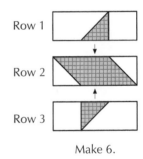

Make 6.

5. Join 3 Star blocks.

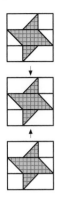

Finishing

1. Referring to the piecing diagram, assemble the star unit, checkerboard strips, and 9½" x 11½" ivory rectangle. Sew the side checkerboard strips to the place mat first, then sew the top and bottom strips to the place mat.

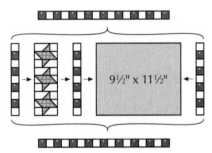

Make 2.

2. Layer the 13½" x 19½" ivory backing, needlepunch, and top, just as you would a quilt. Baste the layers together.
3. Quilt as desired. (See note below.)
4. Trim batting and backing to measure 11½" x 17½".
5. Bind the edges. (See "Binding" on page 16.)

Note: The stencil for quilting design shown can be ordered from Deer Meadow Designs, 130 Lake Drive, Mahopac, New York 10541. (914) 628-5954

Star of Wonder

Photo on page 21
Quilt size: 60" x 75"
Finished block size: 12" x 12"

Materials: 44"-wide fabric

3³/₄ yds. gray print for background
1¹/₄ yds. red print for Stars and Ninepatch
cornerstones

1¹/₂ yds. green print for Star accent, sashing, and
Ninepatch cornerstones
4³/₄ yds. for backing
⁵/₈ yd. for binding

Cutting

Cut strips across the width of the fabric from selvage to selvage unless otherwise noted. Cut narrower strips from the remaining wide strips. Label each set of pieces as you cut them for easy identification.

Fabric	No. of Strips	Strip Width	Piece	No. of Pieces	Dimensions
Gray	2	$1^{1}/_{4}$"	D	48	$1^{1}/_{4}$" x $1^{1}/_{4}$"
	15	$2^{3}/_{4}$"	A	12	$2^{3}/_{4}$" x $2^{3}/_{4}$"
			J	48	$1^{1}/_{4}$" x $2^{3}/_{4}$"
			I	48	$2^{3}/_{4}$" x $3^{1}/_{2}$"
			G	48	$2^{3}/_{4}$" x $6^{1}/_{2}$"
Red	2	$1^{5}/_{8}$"	E	48*	$1^{5}/_{8}$" x $1^{5}/_{8}$"
	8	$2^{3}/_{4}$"	B	108	$2^{3}/_{4}$" x $2^{3}/_{4}$"
	2	5"	K	12	5" x 5"
Green	5	2"	H	96	2" x 2"
	2	$2^{3}/_{8}$"	F	24*	$2^{3}/_{8}$" x $2^{3}/_{8}$"
	2	$2^{3}/_{4}$"	C	24	$2^{3}/_{4}$" x $2^{3}/_{4}$"

*Cut each square in half once diagonally.

Unit Assembly

Note: Follow pressing instructions carefully when piecing each unit. Because there are many points, it is important to accurately press each unit to make block assembly easier. Press seam allowances in the direction of the arrows, unless otherwise noted.

1. Draw an X from corner to corner on the wrong side of each green C. With right sides together, place a green C on top of each of 12 gray A squares and 12 red B squares.

2. With the green squares on top, sew ¼" from the drawn line, starting at the outside edge of the square and sewing to the drawn line as shown. Take care to sew exactly as shown in the diagram, or your triangles will not fit correctly.

3. Cut along the drawn lines. Open the triangle units and press seam allowances away from the green triangle.

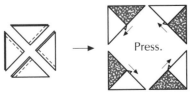

Press.

4. Sew a green-and-red triangle to a green-and-gray triangle to make a 2" x 2" pieced square.

Unit 1
Make 48.

5. Sew a red triangle E to a gray D. Sew a red triangle E to the adjacent side of gray D as shown. Press seam allowances toward the red triangle after sewing each seam. Be careful not to stretch bias edges.

Press.

Make 48.

6. Sew the long side of a green F triangle to the star unit made in step 1 above, making 2" x 2" squares.

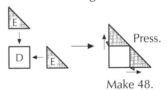

Press.

Unit 2
Make 48.

7. Using the angled-piecing technique on pages 12–13, sew a red B to each end of a gray G. Press seam allowances toward the gray fabric. This unit measures $2^{3}/_{4}$" x $6^{1}/_{2}$".

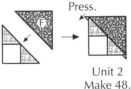

Unit 3
Make 48.

Block Assembly

1. Sew a green H to each side of a Unit 1, matching greens as shown. Press seam allowances away from Unit 1.

Make 48.

2. Sew a Unit 2 to each side of 24 of the units made in step 1, matching greens as shown. Press seam allowances toward each Unit 2.

Make 24.

3. Sew a gray I to each end of 24 of the Unit 3 sections. Press seam allowances toward the gray I rectangles.

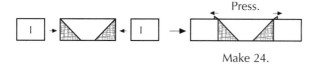

Make 24.

4. Sew a gray J to each end of the 24 remaining Unit 3 sections. Press seam allowances toward the gray J rectangles.

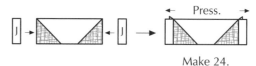

Make 24.

5. Starting with a red K at the center, join the units to make the block. Follow the numerical sequence in the illustration below. Press seam allowances for the center section and units numbered 1, 2, and 3 toward the center. Press seam allowances of units numbered 4–9 away from the center.

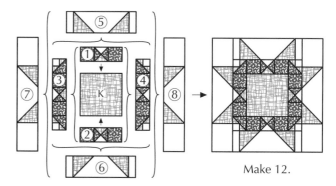

Make 12.

Sashing and Cornerstones

Cutting

Cut strips across the width of the fabric from selvage to selvage.

Fabric	No. of Strips	Strip Width
Gray	24	1½"
Red	4	1½"
Green	11	1½"

Assembly

1. **Sashing Strips:** Sew a gray strip to each side of a green strip.
2. Cut 3 segments, each 12½" long, from each strip made in step 1. Reserve the remaining strip segment to use for cornerstones.

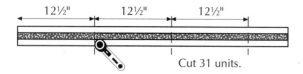

Cut 31 units.

3. **Cornerstones:** Sew a red strip to each side of a gray strip.
4. Cut across each strip-pieced unit at 1½" intervals to make 40 strip-pieced rectangles.

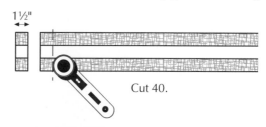

Cut 40.

5. From the remaining strip-pieced sashing segments, cut at 1½" intervals to make 20 strip-pieced rectangles.

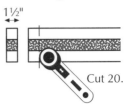

Cut 20.

6. Sew a gray-and-red strip-pieced rectangle to each side of a gray-and-green strip-pieced rectangle to make a cornerstone.

Make 20.

7. Sew a 3½" x 12½" sashing strip to opposite sides of a block. Sew a block to opposite ends of this unit, then sew a sashing strip to each end.

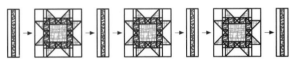

Make 4.

8. Sew a cornerstone between each of 3 sashing strips. Sew a cornerstone to each end of this unit as shown.

9. Sew a sashing row between each block row. Sew rows together, then sew a sashing row to the top and bottom of the quilt.

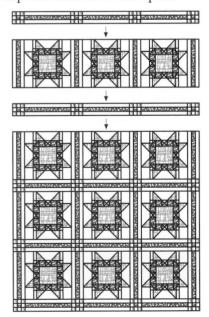

Borders

1. Cut 7 strips, each 1½" wide, from green. Join strips as needed. See "Adding Borders" on page 14 except add side borders first, then top and bottom borders.

Mark centers.

2. For the outer border, cut 8 strips, each 5½" wide, from gray. Join strips as needed. Sew side borders to the quilt, then add top and bottom borders.

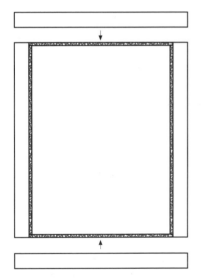

Finishing

1. Layer the quilt with batting and backing. Baste the layers together.
2. Quilt as desired.
3. Cut 8 strips, each 2½" x 44", from the binding fabric. Join strips end to end and bind the quilt. (See "Binding" on page 16.)

Veggies

Photo on page 23
Quilt size: 37½" x 20"
Finished block size: 7½" x 13½"

Materials: 44"-wide fabric

¼ yd. each of four lights for background*
⅛ yd. each of 4 different green prints for leaves
¼ yd. or fat ⅛ yd. each of purple, orange, white,
    and red for veggies
¼ yd. green plaid for accent border and sashing

⅜ yd. dark print for block border
⅜ yd. light print for block border
⅔ yd. for backing
⅓ yd. for binding
White and green embroidery floss

*If you choose 1 background for all four blocks, purchase ½ yard.

Eggplant

Cutting					
Cut strips across the width of the fabric from selvage to selvage unless otherwise noted. Cut narrower strips from the remaining wide strips.					
Fabric	**No. of Strips**	**Strip Width**	**Piece**	**No. of Pieces**	**Dimensions**
Light #1	1	1¼"*	M	1	1¼" x 6½"
			N	1	1¼" x 3¼"
			O	1	1¼" x 2¼"
	1	1½"*	V	1	1½" x 6½"
			C	1	1½" x 4½"
			B	1	1½" x 3½"
			Q	2	1½" x 1½"
			T	1	1" x 1½"
	1	2½"	X	1	2½" x 7½"
			W	1	2" x 7½"
			D	2	2" x 3½"
			S	1	1" x 2"
			G	4	1" x 2"
Green #1	1	2"*	E	1	2" x 4½"
			A	1	1½" x 2½"
			I	1	1" x 3½"
			F	1	1" x 2"
			K	2	1" x 1½"
			L	1	1" x 1"
Purple	1	4½"	R	1	4½" x 6½"
			P	1	1¼" x 3½"
			U	1	1" x 5"
			J	1	1" x 2½"
			H	3	1" x 1½"
*Cut from 22"-long strip					

Assembly

See "Angled Piecing" on pages 12–13.

Assemble eggplant in rows. Rows 1–5 are horizontal and rows 6–10 are vertical. Rows 1, 6, and 10 are light rectangles W, M, and V.

1. Using the angled-piecing technique, sew green A to light B. Sew light C to green A.

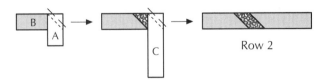

Row 2

2. Using the angled-piecing technique, sew a light D to each end of green E, noting correct angles.

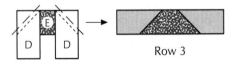

Row 3

3. Using the angled-piecing technique, join pieces from left to right: sew green F to light G, purple H to green F, and green I to purple H. Sew light G to the right side.

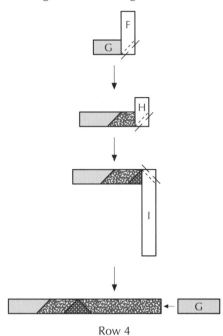

Row 4

4. Sew purple J to a light G. Using the angled-piecing technique, alternate 2 green K and 2 purple H rectangles. Sew green L, then light G to the right side as shown.

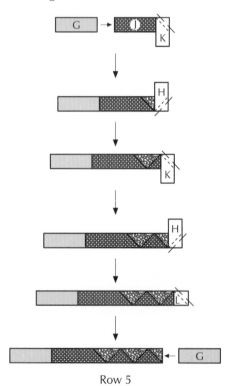

Row 5

5. Using the angled-piecing technique, sew light N to the top and light O to the bottom of purple P, noting correct angles.

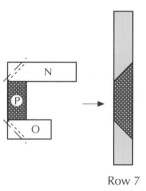

Row 7

6. Using the angled-piecing technique, sew a light Q to each lower corner of purple R.

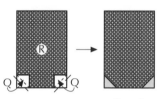

Row 8

7. Using the angled-piecing technique, sew light T to the top and light S to the bottom of purple U as shown.

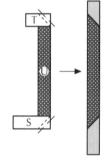

Row 9

8. On a flannel board, arrange horizontal rows 1–5 and vertical rows 6–10. Sew horizontal rows together, then sew vertical rows together. Join these two units, then sew light X to the bottom to complete the Eggplant block.

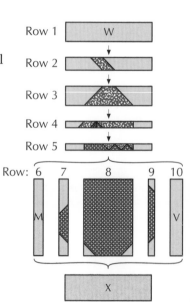

Carrot

Cutting					
Cut strips across the width of the fabric from selvage to selvage unless otherwise noted. Cut narrower strips from the remaining wide strips.					
Fabric	**No. of Strips**	**Strip Width**	**Piece**	**No. of Pieces**	**Dimensions**
Light #2	1	$2^1/_4$"	J	2	$2^1/_4$" x $13^1/_2$"
			B	1	2" x 2"
	1	$1^1/_2$"*	N	1	$1^1/_2$" x 10"
			C	3	$1^1/_2$" x 2"
			F	2	$1^1/_2$" x $1^1/_2$"
	1	$1^1/_4$"	I	2	$1^1/_4$" x $7^1/_2$"
			K	2	1" x 6"
			E	2	1" x 4"
			A	1	1" x 2"
Green #2	1	1"	M	1	1" x 10"
			L	1	1" x 6"
			D	1	1" x $5^1/_2$"
Orange	1	$2^1/_2$"*	G	1	$2^1/_2$" x 6"
			H	1	$1^1/_2$" x 2"
*Cut from 22"- long strip.					

Assembly

See "Angled Piecing" on pages 12–13.

1. Sew a light K lengthwise to each side of green L. Press seam allowances away from the center. Crosscut at 1" intervals to make 4 strip-pieced rectangles.

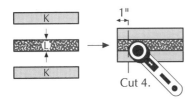

Cut 4.

2. Sew light N to green M. Press seam allowances toward the green strip. Crosscut at 1" intervals to make 8 strip-pieced rectangles.

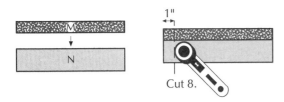

Cut 8.

3. Assemble the strip-pieced segments made in steps 1 and 2 to make 4 carrot-top units as shown.

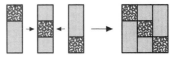

Make 4.

4. On a flannel board, arrange carrot top units, green D, and light pieces A, B, and C to make the carrot-top block. Join the units, then sew a light E across the top.

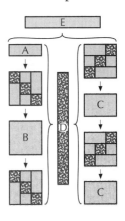

5. Using the angled-piecing technique, sew a light F to orange G.

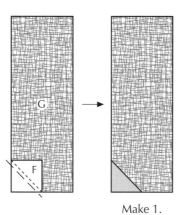

Make 1.

6. Using the angled-piecing technique, sew a light F to orange H. Sew a light C to the left side.

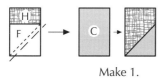

Make 1.

7. Join the two carrot units made in steps 5 and 6, then sew a light I to each side. Sew a light E across the bottom.

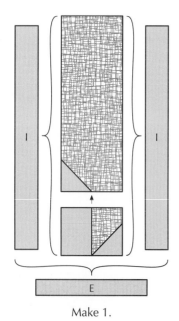

Make 1.

8. Sew the carrot top and carrot units together; sew a light J to each side.

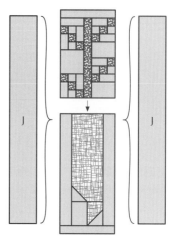

Make 1.

Onion

Cutting					
Cut strips across the width of the fabric from selvage to selvage unless otherwise noted. Cut narrower strips from the remaining wide strips.					
Fabric	**No. of Strips**	**Strip Width**	**Piece**	**No. of Pieces**	**Dimensions**
Light #3	1	1½"*	A	1	1½" x 2½"
			D	6	1½" x 2"
			B	1	1½" x 1½"
	1	7½"*	M	1	1½" x 7½"
			I	1	6¼" x 6¼"
			L	2	3¼" x 5½"
Green #3	1	1½"	H	1	1½" x 5"
			G	2	1½" x 4"
			F	2	1½" x 3"
			E	1	1½" x 2"
			C	2	1⅝" x 1⅝"
	(cut from scrap)		J	1	2" x 3"
White			K	1	2" x 3"
*Cut from 22"-long strip.					

Assembly

See "Angled Piecing" on pages 12–13.

1. Sew light B to a green C. Using the angled-piecing technique, sew a light D to each of green pieces F and G, then sew a light D to each green E and H. Arrange on a flannel board, referring to the illustration in step 3 below. Use the numbers in the illustration below for placement.

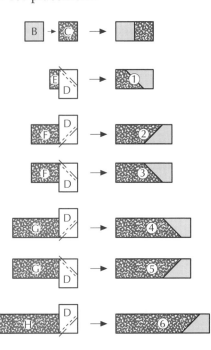

2. Sew Unit 1 to the left side of the B/C unit. Sew light A to the right side as shown.

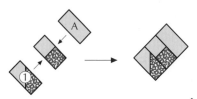

3. Referring to the illustration at right, join units in the numbered order shown.

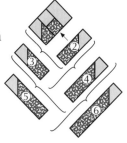

4. Cut light I in half twice diagonally. Sew the long side of a quarter-square triangle to the upper left and right of the onion top.

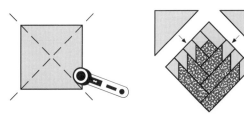

5. Place the 2 remaining triangles with right sides together. Measure $1\frac{1}{8}$" from the lower point and cut off the tip at a 90° angle. Cut a green C in half once diagonally. Sew a short edge of this triangle to the large light triangle as shown.

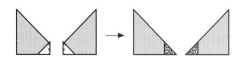

$1\frac{1}{8}$"

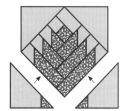

6. Sew the pieced triangles made in step 5 to the onion-top unit.

7. Sew green J to white K, then sew a light L to each side. Sew light M to the bottom.

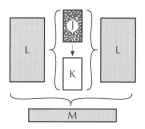

8. Join onion top and lower onion units.

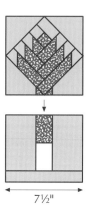

$7\frac{1}{2}$"

Radish

Cutting					
Cut strips across the width of the fabric from selvage to selvage unless otherwise noted. Cut narrower strips from the remaining wide strips.					
Fabric	**No. of Strips**	**Strip Width**	**Piece**	**No. of Pieces**	**Dimensions**
Light #4	1	$1\frac{1}{2}$"	J	2	$1\frac{1}{2}$" x $4\frac{1}{2}$"
			A	2	$1\frac{1}{2}$" x 4"
			C	2	$1\frac{1}{2}$" x 3"
			F	3	$1\frac{1}{2}$" x $2\frac{1}{2}$"
			E	4	$1\frac{1}{2}$" x 2"
			H	2	$1\frac{1}{2}$" x $1\frac{1}{2}$"
	1	$2\frac{1}{2}$"	M	1	$2\frac{1}{2}$" x $7\frac{1}{2}$"
			N	1	2" x $7\frac{1}{2}$"
			L	2	2" x 4"
			G	2	2" x 2"
Green	1	$1\frac{1}{2}$"	B	6	$1\frac{1}{2}$" x $2\frac{1}{2}$"
			D	1	$1\frac{1}{2}$" x $2\frac{1}{2}$"
Red			I	1	$4\frac{1}{2}$" x $5\frac{1}{2}$"
White			K	1	2" x $3\frac{1}{2}$"

Assembly

See "Angled Piecing" on pages 12–13. Assemble radish in horizontal rows; rows 1 and 8 are light rectangles M and N.

1. Using the angled-piecing technique, sew a light A to each end of green B.

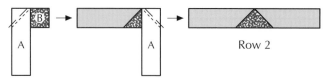

Row 2

2. Sew a light C to each end of green D.

Row 3

3. Using the angled-piecing technique, begin the row with a light E, alternate 3 green B with 2 light F rectangles, and end the row with a light E as shown.

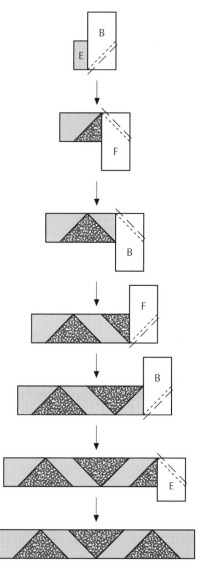

Row 4

4. Using the angled-piecing technique, sew a green B to each end of a light F. Sew a light E to each end of the row.

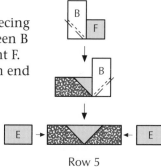

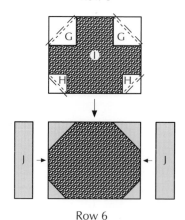

Row 5

5. Using the angled-piecing technique, sew a light G to each upper corner and a light H to each lower corner of red I. Sew a light J to each side.

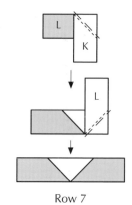

Row 6

6. Use the angled-piecing technique to sew a light L to each end of white K.

7. Join rows 1–8 to make the radish unit.

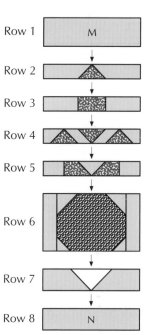

Row 7

73

Quilt Top Assembly

Accent Strips

Cutting				
Cut strips across the width of the fabric from selvage to selvage.				
Fabric	No. of Strips	Strip Width	No. of Pieces	Dimensions
Green plaid	1	$1^1/4$"	2	$1^1/4$" x $13^1/2$"
	3	$1^1/2$"	2	$1^1/2$" x 33"
			3	$1^1/2$" x $13^1/2$"

1. Sew a $1^1/2$" x $13^1/2$" accent strip between each block. Sew a $1^1/4$" x $13^1/2$" strip to each end of the row. Sew a $1^1/2$" x 33" strip to the top and bottom of the quilt.

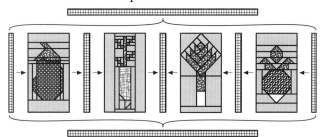

2. Cut 2 strips, each 3" wide, from each of the light and dark border fabrics.
3. Sew a light strip to a dark strip. Cut across each strip-pieced unit at 3" intervals to make strip-pieced rectangles.

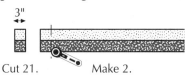

Cut 21.   Make 2.

4. Join all rectangles, end to end, alternating colors to total 42 squares.

5. For each side border, count 6 squares, then remove stitching. With a light square at the top, sew a border to each quilt side.

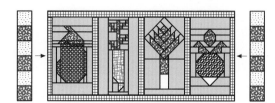

6. For the top border, start with a dark square, count 15 squares, then remove stitching. Sew to the quilt. For the bottom border, start with a light square, count 15 squares, then remove stitching. Sew to the quilt.

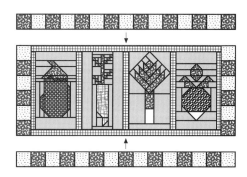

7. Baste around the border to keep the stitching from tearing out while finishing.

Finishing

1. Using a stem stitch, embroider 5 rows of white stitches for onion roots and 1 row of stitches for the radish root. Embroider a row of green stitches for the stem between the upper radish leaf and the radish. (See "Embroidery Stitches" on pages 8–9.)

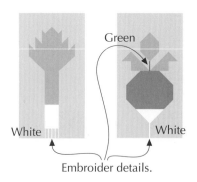

Embroider details.

2. Layer the quilt with batting and backing. Baste the layers together.
3. Quilt as desired.
4. Cut 4 strips, each $2^1/2$" x 44", from the binding fabric. Bind the quilt. (See "Binding" on page 16.)

Garden Fresh in Miniature

Photo on page 23
Quilt size: 22" x 23¹/₂"

Materials: 44"-wide fabric

¹/₄ yd. each of 4 different tans for background
¹/₈ yd. each (or scraps) of 5 greens in dark,
  medium, and light values
¹/₈ yd. orange for carrots
¹/₈ yd. cranberry print for accent border
¹/₄ yd. dark blue print for checkerboard border
¹/₄ yd. light tan print for checkerboard border

³/₄ yd. for backing
¹/₄ yd. for binding
Assorted scraps:
  Red and white for radish
  Yellow for turnip
  Dark, medium, and light purple for asparagus
Green embroidery floss

Tip

For the greens and light, medium, and dark purples, use several different prints to give the asparagus a variegated look.

Radishes

Fabric	No. of Strips	Strip Width	Piece	No. of Pieces	Dimensions
Tan #1	1	1"	G	2	1" x 3½"
			E	4	1" x 6½"
	2	1½"	A	48	1" x 1½"
	1	2"	F	2	2" x 3½"
			H	1	2" x 8½"
Green	1	1½"	B	32	1" x 1½"
Red			C	8	1" x 1½"
White			D	8	1" x 1½"

Cutting

Cut strips across the width of the fabric from selvage to selvage.
Cut narrower strips from the remaining wide strips.

> **Tip**
> Use your flannel board to lay out small pieces (see "Flannel Board" on page 6).

Assembly

1. Following directions on pages 10–12 for making bias-rectangle units, pair tan A rectangles with green B, red C, and white D rectangles. Make the number of right and left bias-rectangle units shown below. Do not press the bias-rectangle units after you have sewn them together.

Tan and green
Make 16 of each.

Tan and red
Make 4 of each.

Tan and white
Make 4 of each.

2. Join the left and right bias-rectangle units as shown to make the radish and radish-top units. Finger-press seams as shown.

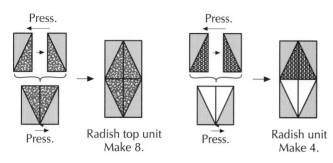

Radish top unit
Make 8.

Radish unit
Make 4.

3. Assemble radish and radish top units as shown to make a 1½" x 6½" radish section.

> **Tip**
> After pressing, if the points are not perfect, try pressing the seam allowances in the opposite direction.

4. On a flannel board, arrange radish sections and tan rectangles E, F, G, and H, referring to the diagram below. Join sections to make an 8" x 8½" block. Press and set aside.

Radish section
Make 4.

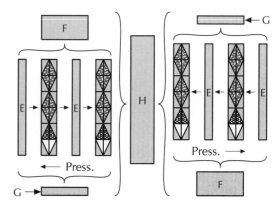

Turnips

Cutting					
Cut strips across the width of the fabric from selvage to selvage unless otherwise noted. Cut narrower strips from the remaining wide strips.					
Fabric	**No. of Strips**	**Strip Width**	**Piece**	**No. of Pieces**	**Dimensions**
Tan #2	1	1"	I	2	1" x 8½"
			H	3	1" x 2½"
			E	6	1" x 1"
	2	1½"	J	2	1½" x 8½"
			A	6	1½" x 5"
			G	3	1½" x 2½"
			C	6	1½" x 2"
Green	1	1½"*	B	3	1½" x 5"
Yellow	1	2"*	D	6	1½" x 2"
			F	3	1" x 2½"
*Cut from 22"- long strip.					

Assembly

Refer to "Bias Rectangles" on pages 10–12 and "Angled Piecing" on pages 12-13.

1. Place each tan A with a green B to make 1 right bias-rectangle unit and 2 left bias-rectangle units. Press seam allowances toward the tan.

Left bias rectangle unit   Right bias rectangle unit

Make 2.   Make 1.

2. To make the turnip tops, sew a tan A to the green triangle of each bias-rectangle unit.

Make 1.   Make 2.

3. Place each tan C with a yellow D to make 3 right bias-rectangle units and 3 left bias-rectangle units. Join each right bias rectangle unit to a left bias-rectangle unit to make the lower turnip.

Right bias rectangle unit   Left bias rectangle unit

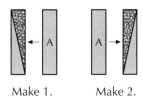

Make 3.   Make 3.   Make 3.

4. Using the angled-piecing technique, sew a tan E to each end of yellow F to make the upper turnip.

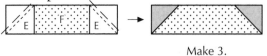

Make 3.

5. Sew the upper turnip to the lower turnip.

Make 3.

6. Sew the turnip section to the turnip-top section to make a 2½" x 7" unit.

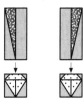

Make 1.   Make 2.

7. On the flannel board, arrange turnip sections and tan rectangles G, H, I, and J, referring to the diagram below and taking care that turnip tops are positioned correctly. Join sections to make a 9½" x 9½" block. Press and set aside.

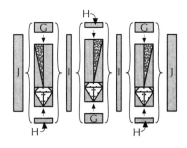

Asparagus

Cutting					
Cut strips 22" long, except where indicated.					
Fabric	**No. of Strips**	**Strip Width**	**Piece**	**No. of Pieces**	**Dimensions**
Tan #3	1	1"	P	1	1" x 3$\frac{1}{2}$"
			N	2	1" x 1$\frac{3}{4}$"
			G	4	1" x 1$\frac{1}{2}$"
			H	2	1" x 1"
	1	2"*	Q	1	2" x 10$\frac{1}{2}$"
			R	1	1$\frac{1}{2}$" x 10$\frac{1}{2}$"
			O	1	1$\frac{1}{2}$" x 3$\frac{1}{2}$"
Dark purple	1	1"	L	2	1" x 1$\frac{3}{4}$"
			A	4	1" x 1$\frac{1}{2}$"
Med. purple	1	1"	B	2	1" x 2$\frac{1}{2}$"
			I	4	1" x 2"
Light purple	1	1"	C	4	1" x 2$\frac{1}{2}$"
Light green	1	1"	M	2	1" x 3"
			D	2	1" x 2"
Med. green	1	1"	J	2	1" x 3"
			E	4	1" x 2$\frac{1}{2}$"
Dark green	1	1"	K	4	1" x 3"
			F	2	1" x 2$\frac{1}{2}$"
*Cut strip 44" long					

Tip

It is easiest to lay pieces on the flannel board as you cut, in the order shown below. Make two of each kind of asparagus stalk. Stack the fabric pairs for each stalk, laying out the pairs in three rows. Each row represents a stalk.

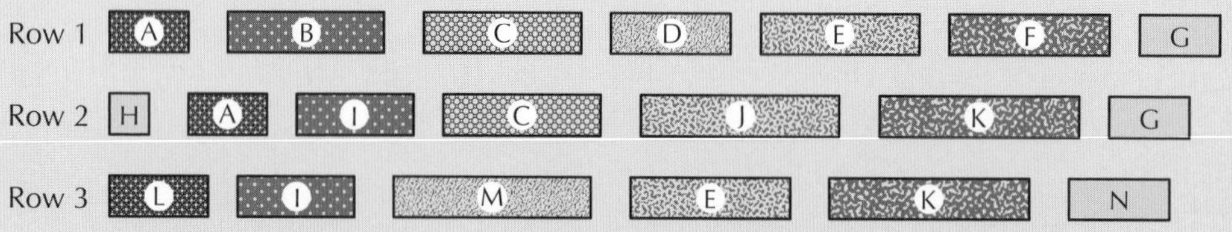

Row 1 A B C D E F G

Row 2 H A I C J K G

Row 3 L I M E K N

Assembly

See "Angled Piecing" on pages 12–13.

1. Using the angled-piecing technique, assemble rows 1–3 as shown below. Press the seam allowances in one direction. Make 2 of each asparagus stalk. Each stalk is 1" x 9".

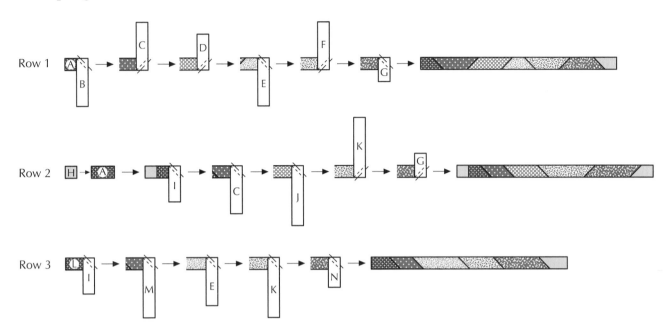

2. Join rows in the order shown below to make a 3½" x 9" section. Press seam allowances to one side.

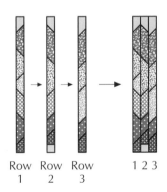

Row   Row   Row
1   2   3   1 2 3

3. On a flannel board, arrange the asparagus section and tan rectangles O–R, referring to the diagram below and taking care that the stalk tips are at the top. Sew together to make a 6" x 10½" block. Press and set aside.

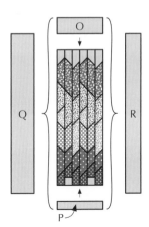

Carrot

Fabric	No. of Strips	Strip Width	Piece	No. of Pieces	Dimensions
		Cutting			
		Cut strips across the width of the fabric from selvage to selvage. Cut narrower strips from the remaining wide strips.			
Tan #4	2	1"	N	1	1" x 10½"
			G	4	1" x 4"
			C	6	1" x 1½"
			A	18	1" x 1"
	1	1½"*	K	1	1½" x 5"
			H	1	1½" x 4"
			I	1	1½" x 2"
			E	6	1½" x 1½"
	1	3"	M	1	3" x 11"
			L	2	2½" x 6½"
			J	1	2" x 5"
Orange	1	2"	B	6	2" x 2"
			D	6	1½" x 1½"
			F	6	1" x 1½"

*Cut from 22"- long strip.

Assembly

Use the angled piecing technique as shown for steps 1–3. See "Angled Piecing" on pages 12–13.

1. Sew a tan A to an orange B.

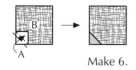

Make 6.

2. Sew a tan A to an orange D, then sew a tan C to the left side.

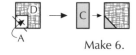

Make 6.

3. Sew a tan A to an orange F, then sew a tan E to the left side.

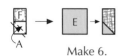

Make 6.

4. Assemble the units made in steps 1–3 to make the 2" x 4" carrot section.

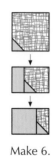

Make 6.

5. Arrange carrot sections and tan rectangles G–L on the flannel board, referring to the diagram below. Join units, then sew tan M to the top. Sew tan N to the left side to make an 11½" x 10½" block. Press and set aside.

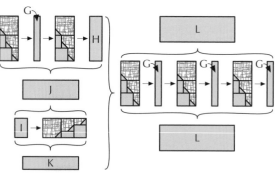

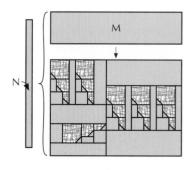

Accent Border

Cutting				
Cut strips across the width of the fabric from selvage to selvage.				
Fabric	**No. of Strips**	**Strip Width**	**No. of Pieces**	**Dimensions**
Cranberry	3	1"	1	1" x 8¹/₂"
			1	1" x 10¹/₂"
			3	1" x 17¹/₂"
			2	1" x 20"

Assembly

1. Sew the 1" x 8¹/₂" strip between the radish and turnip sections. Sew the 1" x 10¹/₂" strip between the asparagus and carrot sections. Sew a 1" x 17¹/₂" strip between the 2 vegetable sections and to the top and bottom edges.

2. Sew a 1" x 20" strip to the left and right sides to make an 18¹/₂" x 20" quilt top.

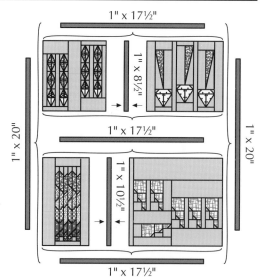

Checkerboard Border

Cutting				
Cut strips across the width of the fabric from selvage to selvage. *Cut narrower strips from the remaining wide strips.*				
Fabric	**No. of Strips**	**Strip Width**	**No. of Pieces**	**Dimensions**
Dark Blue print	3	1¹/₂"		1¹/₂" x 44"
Tan	3	1¹/₂"		1¹/₂" x 44"
	1	2¹/₂"	2	2¹/₂" x 2¹/₂"
			3	2¹/₂" x 3"
			3	2¹/₂" x 4"

Assembly

1. Join 1¹/₂" x 44" dark blue and tan strips. Press seam allowances toward the dark blue strip. Crosscut at 1¹/₂" intervals to make 1¹/₂" x 2¹/₂" rectangles.

2. Join units to form a checkerboard. Press seam allowances in one direction.

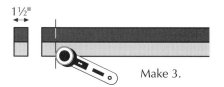

Make 3.

3. For borders, make checkerboard sections according to the illustration below. Remove stitching between units to make the sections needed.

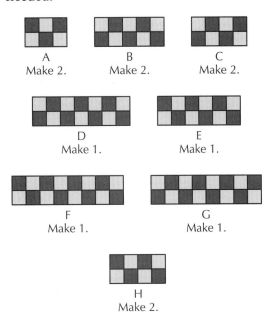

A
Make 2.

B
Make 2.

C
Make 2.

D
Make 1.

E
Make 1.

F
Make 1.

G
Make 1.

H
Make 2.

Adding Borders

1. Assemble top, bottom, and side borders by alternating checkerboard sections with tan pieces as indicated in the diagram below. Top and bottom borders measure $18\frac{1}{2}$" x $2\frac{1}{2}$". Side borders measure $2\frac{1}{2}$" x 24".

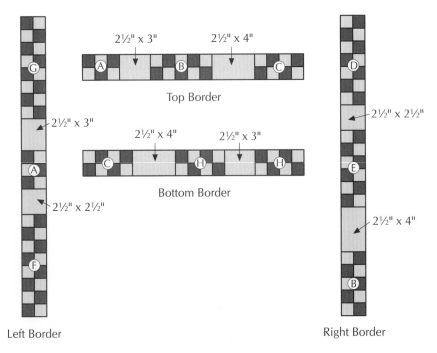

2½" x 3"   2½" x 4"

Top Border

2½" x 4"   2½" x 3"

Bottom Border

2½" x 3"

2½" x 2½"

Left Border

2½" x 2½"

2½" x 4"

Right Border

2. Sew top and bottom borders to the quilt top first, then add side borders.

Finishing

1. Using the stem stitch, embroider carrot tops with green floss. (See "Embroidery Stitches" on pages 8–9.)

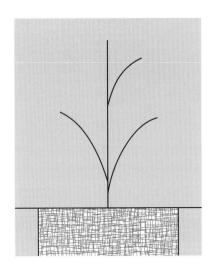

Carrot Top Template

2. Layer the quilt with batting and backing. Baste the layers together.
3. Quilt as desired.
4. Cut 4 strips, each $2\frac{1}{2}$" x 44", from the binding fabric. Bind the quilt. (See "Binding" on page 16.)

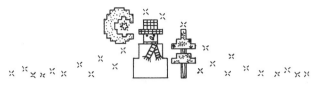

Winter Evening

Photo on page 17
Quilt size: 36¹⁄₂" x 33"

Materials: 44"-wide fabric

2 yds. black for background and outer border
¹⁄₈ yd. brown for trunks
¹⁄₄ yd. dark green for large tree
¹⁄₄ yd. medium green for small trees
¹⁄₈ yd. gold for moon
¹⁄₄ yd. white for snowman
¹⁄₈ yd. blue for hat
¹⁄₈ yd. red #1 for scarf

Assorted yellow scraps for stars
¹⁄₂ yd. red #2 for accent border and binding
53 buttons in various sizes and colors for trees
Carrot button for nose (or make carrot nose, using orange fabric with fusible web)
2 buttons, each ¹⁄₄", for snowman's eyes
Paper-backed fusible web
Blue embroidery floss for tassels on scarf

Tree Trunks

1. From black, cut 2 strips, each 3½" x 44". From brown, cut 1 strip, 1½" x 44".

2. Sew a black strip to each side of the brown strip. Press seam allowances away from center.

Press.

3. From the strip-pieced unit, cut rectangles in the following amounts and widths to make units A–D:

Unit	No. of Pieces	Unit Width
A	3	1¼"
B	4	1½"
C	2	3½"
D	1	8"

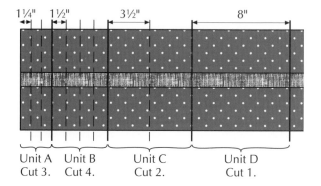

| 1¼" | 1½" | 3½" | 8" |

Unit A Unit B Unit C Unit D
Cut 3. Cut 4. Cut 2. Cut 1.

Large Tree

Cutting				
Cut strips across the width of the fabric from selvage to selvage. *Cut narrower strips from the remaining wide strips.*				
Fabric	**No. of Strips**	**Strip Width**	**No. of Pieces**	**Dimensions**
Black (Note: If your background fabric is narrower than 44", cut one more strip for each width.)				
	1	1½"	2	1½" x 10"
	2	2½"	2	2½" x 10"
			2	2½" x 3½"
			1	2" x 7½"
Dark green	1	5½"	1	5½" x 10"
			1	3½" x 10"
			1	1½" x 2½"

Assembly

1. Sew a 2¹/₂" x 10" black strip to each side of the 3¹/₂" x 10" dark green strip. Press seam allowances away from the center.

2. From this strip, cut at 1¹/₂" intervals to make 5 strip-pieced rectangles.

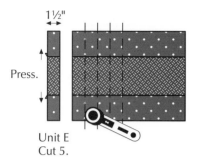

1¹/₂"

Press.

Unit E
Cut 5.

3. Sew a 1¹/₂" x 10" black strip to each side of the 5¹/₂" x 10" dark green strip. Press seam allowances away from the center.

4. From this strip, cut at 1¹/₂" intervals to make 5 strip-pieced rectangles.

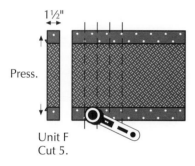

1¹/₂"

Press.

Unit F
Cut 5.

5. Sew a Unit B and a Unit F to each side of a Unit E. Press seam allowances toward Unit B.

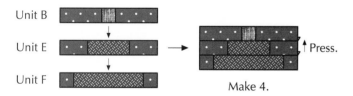

Unit B

Unit E

Unit F

Press.

Make 4.

6. Sew a Unit F to a Unit E. Sew a 2¹/₂" x 3¹/₂" black rectangle to each side of a 1¹/₂" x 2¹/₂" green rectangle. Sew this unit to the top of unit E/F.

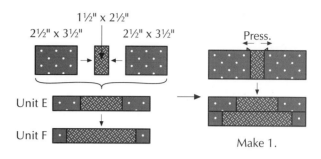

1¹/₂" x 2¹/₂"

2¹/₂" x 3¹/₂"   2¹/₂" x 3¹/₂"

Press.

Unit E

Unit F

Make 1.

7. Join units, referring to the diagram. Sew the unit made in step 6 to the top. Sew Unit D to the bottom of the tree. Sew the 2" x 7¹/₂" black rectangle to the top to make the 7¹/₂" x 25¹/₂" tree section. Press all seam allowances toward the top of the tree and set aside. The unfinished block size is 7¹/₂" x 25¹/₂".

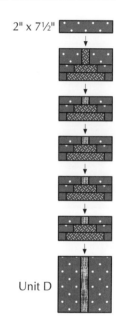

2" x 7¹/₂"

Unit D

Medium and Small Trees

Cutting				
Cut strips across the width of the fabric from selvage to selvage unless otherwise noted. Cut narrower strips from the remaining wide strips.				
Fabric	**No. of Strips**	**Strip Width**	**No. of Pieces**	**Dimensions**
Black	1	$6^3/_4$"	1	$6^3/_4$" x $14^1/_2$"
			1	$2^3/_4$" x $7^1/_2$"
			4	$1^1/_4$" x $3^1/_2$"
	1	$1^1/_2$"*	2	$1^1/_2$" x 10"
	1	$2^1/_2$"*	2	$2^1/_2$" x 10"
Med. green	2	$5^1/_2$"	1	$5^1/_2$" x 10"
			1	$3^1/_2$" x 10"
			2	$1^1/_4$" x $1^1/_2$"
*Cut from 22"-long strip.				

Assembly

1. Sew a $2^1/_2$" x 10" black strip to each side of the $3^1/_2$" x 10" medium green strip. Press seam allowances away from the center.

2. Crosscut this strip-pieced unit at $1^1/_4$" intervals to make 5 strip-pieced rectangles.

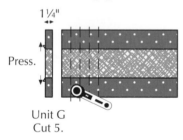

1¼"

Press.

Unit G
Cut 5.

3. Sew a $1^1/_2$" x 10" black strip to each side of the $5^1/_2$" x 10" medium green strip. Press seam allowances away from the center.

4. Crosscut this strip-pieced unit at $1^1/_4$" intervals to make 5 strip-pieced rectangles.

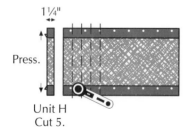

1¼"

Press.

Unit H
Cut 5.

5. Sew a Unit A and a Unit H to each side of a Unit G. Use 2 of these units in the medium tree. Press seam allowances toward Unit H. Use the remaining unit for the small tree. Press seam allowances toward Unit A.

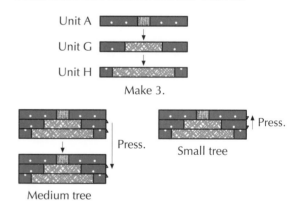

Unit A

Unit G

Unit H

Make 3.

Press.

Medium tree

Press.

Small tree

6. Sew a Unit G to a Unit H. Sew 1 of these units to the top of each tree. Press all seam allowances for the medium tree toward the bottom of the tree. Press all seam allowances for the small tree toward the top of the tree.

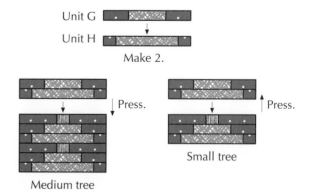

Unit G

Unit H

Make 2.

Press.

Medium tree

Press.

Small tree

7. Sew a 1¼" x 3½" black rectangle to each side of a 1¼" x 1½" green rectangle. Sew to the top of each tree. Add a Unit C to the bottom of each tree. Sew a 2¾" x 7½" black rectangle to the top of the small tree. Each tree unit measures 7½" x 10¼".

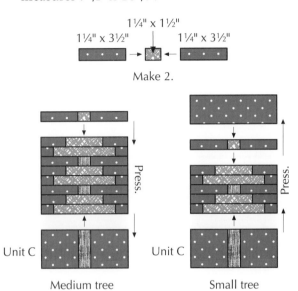

1¼" x 1½"

1¼" x 3½"   1¼" x 3½"

Make 2.

Press.

Press.

Unit C   Unit C

Medium tree   Small tree

8. Join the medium and small trees. Add the 6¾" x 14½" black piece to the top. The unfinished block size is 10½" x 14½".

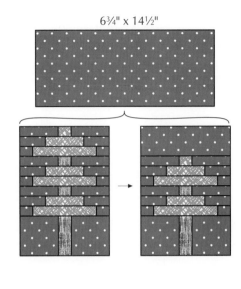

6¾" x 14½"

Moon

Fabric	No. of Strips	Strip Width	Piece	No. of Pieces	Dimensions
		Cutting			
Black	1	1"*	C	2	1" x 5½"
			A	2	1" x 4½"
	2	1½"	R	1	1½" x 8"
			F	2	1½" x 4½"
			M	1	1½" x 4"
			D	5	1½" x 3½"
			G	2	1½" x 2½"
			K	2	1½" x 2"
			I	2	1½" x 1½"
	1	2½"*	S	1	2½" x 9½"
			Q	1	2½" x 8½"
			O	1	2" x 2½"
Gold	1	1½"	E	2	1½" x 5½"
			H	2	1½" x 4½"
			L	2	1½" x 3½"
			J	2	1½" x 2½"
			N	1	1½" x 1½"
			B	2	1" x 3½"
			P	1**	2½" x 3"

Cut strips across the width of the fabric from selvage to selvage unless otherwise noted.
Cut narrower strips from the remaining wide strips. Label cut pieces with letters for easy identification.

*Cut from 22"-long strip.
**Cut from scrap.

Assembly

1. On a flannel board, arrange and assemble gold and black pieces in rows, referring to the diagram below. (See "Flannel Board" on page 6.) Join rows. Press seam allowances toward the top of the moon.

2. To complete the moon section, add black S to the right side. The unfinished block size is 14½" x 9½".

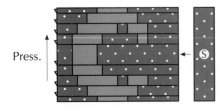

Press.

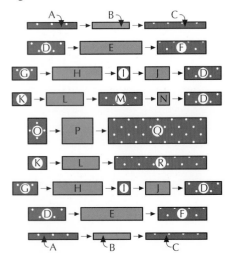

Snowman

Cutting					

Cut strips across the width of the fabric from selvage to selvage unless otherwise noted.
Cut narrower strips from the remaining wide strips. Label cut pieces with letters for easy identification.

Fabric	No. of Strips	Strip Width	Piece	No. of Pieces	Dimensions
Black	1 rectangle		L	1	$9^1/_2$" x $12^1/_2$"
	1	$3^1/_2$"	E	2	3" x $3^1/_2$"
			A	4	$2^1/_2$" x $3^1/_2$"
			C	2	$1^1/_2$" x $2^1/_2$"
			I	2	$1^1/_2$" x $4^1/_2$"
	1	$1^1/_2$"	M	1	$1^1/_2$" x $30^1/_2$"
White	1	$4^1/_2$"*	J	1	$4^1/_2$" x $7^1/_2$"
			H	1	$3^1/_2$" x $5^1/_2$"
			F	1	$2^1/_2$" x $3^1/_2$"
Blue	1	$2^1/_2$"*	B	1	$2^1/_2$" x $3^1/_2$"
			D	1	$1^1/_2$" x $5^1/_2$"
Red #1	1	$2^1/_2$"*	K	2	$2^1/_2$" x 4"
			G	1	1" x $3^1/_2$"

*Cut from 22"-long strip or cut from scraps.

Assembly

1. Fold each red K piece in half lengthwise with right sides together. With a $^1/_4$"-wide seam allowance, sew each piece along the long side and across one end. Turn through the opening and press.

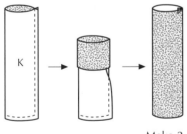

Make 2.

2. Take a small tuck in each red piece at the open end by placing the fold line along the dotted line and pinning or basting the tuck in place. Pin both red pieces together so that the tails are at an angle; baste across the top.

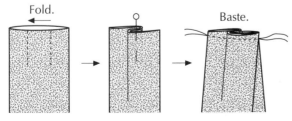

Fold.   Baste.

3. Pin the unfinished edges of the scarf to the right side of red G leaving a $^1/_4$" wide seam allowance, then stitch white F and red G together, catching the edges of the scarf. Press seam allowances toward white F.

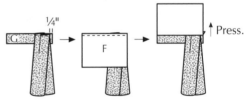

4. Referring to the diagram, arrange pieces in horizontal rows on the flannel board. Sew pieces into rows and join rows. The unfinished block size is 9" x $25^1/_2$".

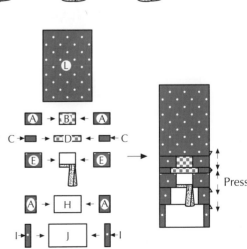

5. Sew the medium-and-small trees section to the moon section. Sew the snowman section to the large tree section. Join these 2 sections, then sew black M across the top.

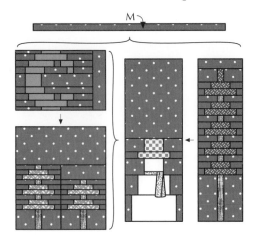

Borders

1. From red #2, cut 2 strips, each 1¹/₂" x 30¹/₂". Sew strips to the top and bottom of the quilt. Cut 2 strips, each 1¹/₂" x 28"; sew one strip to each side of the quilt top.
2. From black, cut 2 strips, each 3" x 32¹/₂". Sew strips to the top and bottom of the quilt. Cut 2 strips, each 3" x 33"; sew one strip to each side of the quilt top.

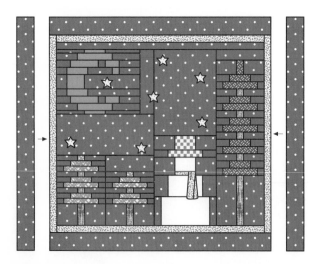

Finishing

1. Trace the star pattern onto paper-backed fusible web to make 7 stars. Referring to the quilt plan on page 83, arrange stars on the background fabric and fuse in place, following the manufacturer's instructions.

Star
Cut 7

2. Sew 3 buttons on each 5¹/₂"-long tree branch, 2 buttons on each 3¹/₂"-long tree branch, and 1 button at the top of each tree.

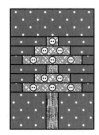

3. Sew ¹/₄" button eyes and carrot nose to the snowman. Embroider or quilt a smile.

4. Using 6 strands of blue embroidery floss, sew fringe on scarf. Tie 3 square knots across scarf ends. Cut ends 1" long.

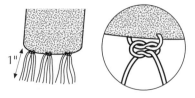

1"

5. Sew 9 tiny buttons or french knots down the center of the snowman, and add any touches you think will make your snowman smile.
6. Layer the quilt with batting and backing. Baste the layers together.
7. Quilt as desired.
8. For binding, cut 4 strips, each 2¹/₂" x 44", from red #2. Bind the quilt. (See "Binding" on page 16.)

Canvas Floorcloths

General Directions

Canvas floorcloths are colorful alternatives to rugs. They are long wearing, easy to care for, and add a warm and personal atmosphere to any decor. Floorcloths were one of the primary floor coverings before the advent of linoleum.

Anyone can make a floorcloth. Use any of the project designs in this book for inspiration, or buy stencils.

A general materials list appears at right. Each floorcloth project includes the paint colors and specific size of canvas needed. Purchase the floorcloth supplies from your local craft store. If you can't find the canvas width you need, sew strips of canvas together using a ⅝"-wide seam allowance. Finger-press the seam open and glue the seam allowance flat with tacky glue.

Always use a good quality acrylic paint for your design. (I used Ceramcoat® by Delta.) Use masking tape to create clean straight lines, checks, and stripes. Consider sponge-painting large areas or backgrounds. Try making designs with hand prints and spattered paint.

Use good quality synthetic brushes made for use with acrylics. Be sure they are in good shape. Use a liner brush for line work. If you are not comfortable using a brush for line work, use a permanent-ink pen instead. If you use a permanent-ink pen, let the ink dry for twenty-four hours before applying clear varnish. Test a small patch with the varnish to make sure the ink does not smear. I use a light coat of spray varnish to set the ink and then brush on the varnish.

It is important to keep brushes clean. Keep a brush basin, half full of water, handy at all times. A brush basin is a square plastic container, 4" deep, with indentations to hold brushes on the lip. A margarine tub works if you do not have a brush basin.

Wash brushes thoroughly with cold water before changing colors and wash them out well with soap and water when you finish painting. (I use liquid dishwashing soap.) Never let brushes stand in water. Keep brushes slightly wet so the paint flows onto the canvas smoothly. To do this, dip the brush in water and dab out the excess on paper toweling, then dip in paint.

Sponge painting is effective on large surfaces. To sponge paint, use a porous, dry sponge. Dip it into the paint and sponge excess onto paper until the sponge is almost dry. Then sponge the paint onto the canvas until the intensity of the color fades. Re-dip the sponge in the paint and repeat the process until finished. Use one color or several different colors. While the paint is still wet, use moistened cotton swabs to remove any unwanted paint.

After painting the floorcloth, let it dry completely. This takes approximately three to four hours. After drying, protect the finish with one or two coats of clear varnish. (I use JW's Right Step water base, satin or matte finish.)

Keep finished floorcloths in place with double-sided carpet tape.

As always, sign and date your work.

Materials

1" grid paper for enlarging patterns
Acrylic brushes— #10 flat, #4 flat, and 10-0 liner
Acrylic paints
Ball-point pen or stylus
Black permanent-ink pen, size .05
Clear (nonyellowing) varnish
Cotton swabs
Graphite carbon or white transfer paper
Gray gum eraser
Masking tape (Use 1"-wide masking tape for all-
 purpose work. Use different widths as desired.)
Odorless turpentine
Paper towels
Plastic-coated palette paper or wax paper
Canvas floorcloth, bought already coated with
 gesso (a primer painted on the canvas to prepare
 it for painting)
Sharp pencil
Tacky glue
Tracing paper

Preparing the Canvas

1. Cut the canvas according to the size indicated on the pattern.
2. On the front side of the canvas, draw a pencil line 1" inside the edge on all four sides.

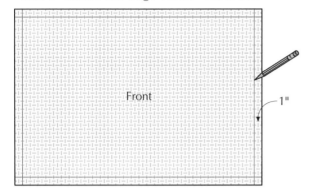

Front

1"

3. On the back, fold each corner down, folding at a 45° angle at the pencil line drawn in step 1. Glue down.

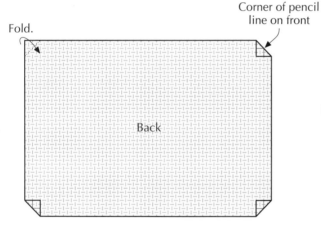

Fold.

Corner of pencil line on front

Back

4. Crease the canvas by folding to the back side on the drawn line. (It is easiest to fold with the back side up.) Spread a thin coat of glue, approximately ³⁄₄" wide, in a circular motion within the 1"-wide margin. Let the glue stand a few minutes until it becomes tacky and press the canvas in place. The corners should form a miter. Press down occasionally until the glue holds.

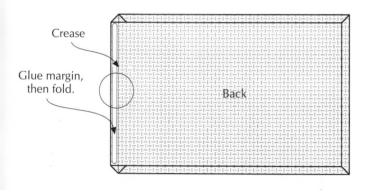

Crease

Glue margin, then fold.

Back

Transferring Patterns

1. Use a sponge brush or a 1" to 1¹⁄₂" soft bristle brush for base-coating. Dip your brush in paint (do not use water) and apply with long, smooth strokes. Apply two coats.
2. Trace the pattern onto a piece of tracing paper. Position the tracing-paper pattern on the prepared surface and hold it in place with masking tape or pressure (I set books on the edges). Slip the graphite or white transfer paper under the pattern. Check to see that you have the coated side down so it will transfer correctly. Draw along the main lines of the design with a ball-point pen or stylus. Do not press so hard that you leave indentations, as they will be visible after you complete the project.

Tip

Use white or very old graphite transfer paper whenever possible. Your goal is to make the tracing clear enough to see but light enough that the paint easily covers it.

Tip

At first, trace only the major areas to be painted. Transfer detail lines after painting these areas. It is usually easier to draw stripes, dots, and stars freehand on smaller areas. If you prefer to trace all the little details, transfer them with white transfer paper. Remove any transfer lines or smudges right away with odorless turpentine on a soft cloth.

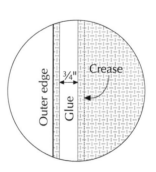

Outer edge

Glue

³⁄₄"

Crease

Cats' Night Out

Photo: Page 20
Size: 26" x 20"

Materials

28" x 22" canvas
Tracing paper
Graphite transfer paper
Sharp pencil
Acrylic brushes— #10 flat, #4 flat, and 10-0 liner
Sponge
Permanent-ink pen

Ceramcoat acrylic paint colors:
  Trail
  Georgia Clay
  Straw
  Territorial Beige
  Cadet Gray
  Black
  Hippo Gray
Clear varnish (nonyellowing)

Directions

1. Prepare the canvas, following the directions given on page 92.
2. Using "Trail" paint, lightly sponge the entire background surface.
3. After the paint has dried, draw a parallel line 2" from the outside edges for the piano-key border.

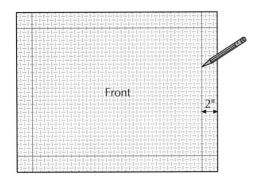

Front

2"

4. Paint the 2"-wide border with "Georgia Clay." Paint two coats with a #10 flat brush. Let the paint dry between coats.

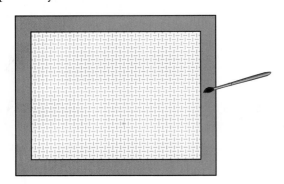

Paint border.

5. Draw the 1"-wide "piano key" stripes. Draw 26 stripes across the top and bottom and 16 stripes on the sides. Paint alternating stripes black. Refer to the photo on page 20 for color placement.

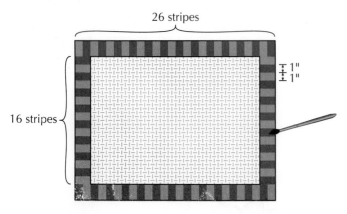

26 stripes

16 stripes

1"
1"

6. Using the star, moon, and cat patterns on the pullout pattern insert, transfer the designs to tracing paper. Remember to reverse one cat. (Refer to "Transferring Patterns" on page 92.) Trace the pattern onto the floorcloth. Refer to the graphed diagram for placement.

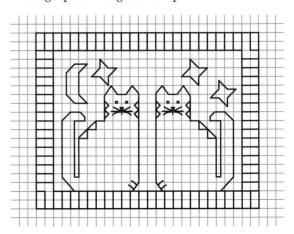

1 square = 1"

7. Paint the cats, moon, and stars with 2 to 3 coats of paint. Refer to the chart below for paint colors.

Design	Primary Color	Accent Color
Moon	Straw	
Stars	Georgia Clay	
Cat (at left)	Territorial Beige	Black
Cat (at right)	Cadet Gray*	Hippo Gray

*Sponge black lightly on top of Cadet Gray when paint is dry.

8. With a liner brush or permanent-ink pen, draw face, leg, paw, and running-stitch lines.
9. Let dry and apply two coats of varnish.

Veggies from the Garden

Photo: page 24
Size: 48" x 24"

Materials

50" x 26" piece of canvas
Tracing paper
Graphite transfer paper
Sharp pencil
Acrylic brushes— #10 flat, #4 flat, and 10-0 liner

Ceramcoat acrylic paint colors:
    Christmas Green
    Trail
    Vintage Wine
    Georgia Clay
    White
    Tomato Spice
Clear varnish (nonyellowing)

Directions

1. Prepare the canvas, following the directions on page 92.
2. Draw a parallel line 2" from the outside edges for the outer border. Paint the 2"-wide border with two coats of "Christmas Green."

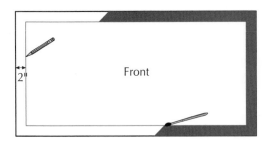

3. Draw a parallel line 4" from the outer border. Mark 2" grid squares inside this border to make a checkerboard. Paint alternating squares "Christmas Green" and leave remaining squares unpainted.

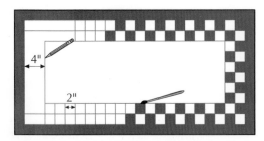

4. Paint the inside rectangle "Trail."

5. For the veggie sections, refer to the diagram below for section divider placement. Draw the 1"-wide section dividers and paint with "Christmas Green."

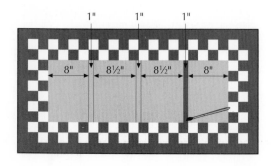

6. Transfer the eggplant, carrot, onion, and radish patterns from the pullout pattern to tracing paper. Place the tracing-paper pattern on the floorcloth and transfer the veggie patterns to their appropriate sections. (Refer to "Transferring Patterns" on page 92.)

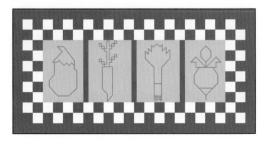

7. Paint the veggies with 2 to 3 coats of color, painting each veggie top "Christmas Green." Refer to the chart below for veggie color placement.

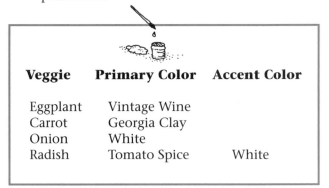

Veggie	Primary Color	Accent Color
Eggplant	Vintage Wine	
Carrot	Georgia Clay	
Onion	White	
Radish	Tomato Spice	White

8. When paint is dry, draw onion roots, radish root, and stitching lines with liner brush or permanent-ink marker. Refer to the pullout pattern insert for line details.
9. Allow to dry and apply two coats of varnish.